NATIONAL

SUNDAY

LAW

A. Jan Marcussen

NATIONAL SUNDAY LAW

A. Jan Marcussen

130th printing - 2018
43.8 million in print

AT Publications
P. O. Box 68
Thompsonville, IL 62890
©1983

The Two Horned Beast 1

The nation trembles. Passenger jets explode into buildings. Mountains of fire, steel, smoke; and terrified, struggling people, fall to the street together as skyscrapers crumble in the dust. Thousands perish. America is at war. A new kind of war fills our minds with pictures of strange faces, balls of fire, women screaming. Dust-filled people - like mummies - running from the cloud, jam the bridges.

"We're at war," the President said. The world will never be the same. Will terrorism, like some giant octopus engulf the world? Or will World War Three end it all!

We're going to go now on an incredible journey behind the scenes and take a shocking glimpse.

Something's happening in our country. Something strange. Have you noticed the trends?

"Thirty-eight people looking out their windows in a quiet, respectable neighborhood of New York City, watched a murder that took a full half hour to commit, and did nothing about it!

"Thirty-eight people watched Catherine Genovese being stabbed again and again in front of her home, and didn't care. They just leaned out their windows as if watching the late show, waited 'till it was over, and went back to bed!"[1]

Since America was attacked, are things different now? Get ready for a shock. You're going to go behind the scenes, and see awesome things that are happening - leading to a great crisis in our land.

It all starts on a stark, rocky island. Into the horizon stretches the vast expanse of the murky deep. One lone figure rests on a barren ledge of sheer rock. His name, John the Revelator. What he sees is fantastic! Strange beasts. Clashing armies. Nations rising.

It's no surprise that the greatest nation on earth should be mentioned in prophecy. What John sees portends events shaping up in the United States that most definitely will affect you!

Watch closely now as the scene unfolds.

"And I beheld another beast coming up out of the earth; and he had two horns like a lamb, and he spake as a dragon." Revelation 13:11. A "beast" in prophecy represents a "kingdom." Daniel 7:23.

When a beast comes up out of the "sea," it is represented in prophecy as rising amid many "peoples and multitudes," {a highly populated area}

2

Revelation 17:15. To come out of the "earth" is just the opposite. So here we have a nation that is springing up out of a wilderness area. Instead of overthrowing vast and well-trained armies from the dense populations of the old world, this nation would be an area "discovered." In the eyes of the "known world," it would be new territory. Differing from the often blood-soaked nations of Europe, it would spring up quietly, peacefully, "like a lamb."

Can you guess what nation of the "new world" arose into power, giving promise of strength and greatness that would fit this description?

Sure! The United States.

It sprang up like a plant from the ground. A prominent author from a hundred years ago, speaks of "the mystery of her coming forth from vacancy," and adds, "like a silent seed we grew into an empire."[2] The pilgrims and settlers met up with the Indian tribes, but compared to the crowded cities and millions of the old world, America was a wilderness.

"And he had two horns like a lamb,"

The lamb-like horns indicate youth, gentleness, and represent civil and religious freedom. The Declaration of Independence and the Constitution reflect these noble views. Because of these very principles, our nation became great. The oppressed and persecuted from all lands have looked to the U.S. with hope.[3]

But the beast with the lamb-like horns "spake as a dragon. And he exerciseth all the power of the first beast before him, and causeth the earth and them which dwell therein to worship the first beast, whose deadly wound was healed. And he doeth great wonders, so that he maketh fire come down from heaven on the earth in the sight of men." Revelation 13:11-13.

Incredible! Keep your eyes open. As the drama unfolds, you will see miracles of a most amazing nature!

". . . Saying to them that dwell on the earth, that they should make an image to the beast, which had the wound by a sword, and did live." Revelation 13:14. Can you imagine the U.S. doing anything like that?!

How could it possibly happen?

Watch closely!

The lamb-like horns and then the dragon voice present a change of personality. A real change! The speaking of this country as a "dragon" denotes the use of force. This principle, as we shall see, was used by the leopard-like beast (the first beast) of Revelation 13, which enforced religious observances by law! Such action by the U.S. government would be directly contrary to its grand principles of religious freedom. The Constitution provides that "Congress shall make no law respecting an establishment of religion, or prohibiting the free exercise thereof."

"Speak as a dragon"- our nation? Do you hear it stirring? Have you noticed attitudes becoming more intolerant and angry lately - angry at crime, terrorism; political, religious, and social corruption?

In view of the horrifying trends of the time, it's understandable why the nation is to "speak" that way. In one year, Americans spent $4 billion on pornography. Mass murders, neglect of the aged, abuse of women and even of babies, sickens the heart. Men possessed are taking the lives of men, women, and little children. Millions of Americans, hooked on marijuana, "crack," heroin, and other chemicals, peer at the world through

4

differing degrees of "goony eyes," and further appall society with their resultant behavior and crimes.

A recent report to the Federal Communications Commission states, "Between the ages of 5 and 14 the average American child witnesses the violent destruction of thirteen thousand human beings on television."[4]

A U.S. senate subcommittee revealed that in one decade violence witnessed on T.V. skyrocketed and delinquency in real life grew nearly 200%![5]

Movies and internet garbage too horrible to mention fill the minds of young and old. Prostitutes, homosexuals, and drug addicts share AIDS with the innocent. The poor sufferers give groans of despair as they perish in ever greater numbers. A group of them, LIFE magazine reported, lying on the floor in a circle, and summoning some of their last remaining strength - laughed in sequence.[6]

In the words of one commentator, "Surely America stumbles headlong toward the final precipice. Tripped on the downward road of immorality, it plunges with ever-increasing momentum toward the point of no return."[7]

Crime doubles every ten years.

Political and religious corruption have caused even the Constitution to come under attack! People are angry. The nation is angry. The shifting of values and anger of the times (in speedy fulfillment of prophecy) are echoed in words blurted out by a Jesuit priest - "I just don't understand the reverence which everybody here seems to pay to the 'Americun Constitushun,' I want to hear some American get up and shout, Give us justice. Give us decency. And to . . . with the American Constitution."

Is it any wonder that our nation will "speak as a dragon?" Little wonder that ministers across the land, in an effort to abort national doom, move millions to political action. The feeling is that something must be done. Leaders of the "electronic church" launched a campaign to arouse 50 million Christians! There's a tremendous drive on to unite forces for the common good.

Pat Robertson said, "Unless Christians desire a nation and a world reordered to the humanistic model; it is absolutely vital that we take control of the U.S. government away from the Trilateral Commission and the Council on Foreign Relations." He speaks of turning to God "to galvanize Christians to political action."[8]

U.S. News & World Report declared, "A political holy war without precedent is in full swing in this country."[9]

The feeling is being spread that only if our nation comes back to God can we improve our sorry state of affairs. Leaders are saying that this can be accomplished if Christians unite. Robert Grant, leader of "Christian Voice" urged: "If Christians unite, we can do anything. We can pass any law or any amendment. And that's exactly what we intend to do." On nationwide T.V. he declared: "We can do anything, we can amend the Constitution. We can elect a president. We can change or make any law in the land. And it behooves us to do it. If we have to live under law, as well we should, we should live under moral and godly law."[10] This is not the opinion of just one man. In a letter written to the leader of the "Religious Roundtable" he was asked if it is time for someone to influence legislation to make Sunday a day of worship in our country.

In reply, the executive director, H. Edward Rowe wrote, "Legislation and proclamations by Presidents to URGE IT, YES!"[11]

The dynamics make us wonder little that nationwide papers and media messages have pled to the masses that it is the responsibility of government to decree the establishment of the national observance of Sunday, and that there will be no relief from mounting economic disaster until a national Sunday law is strictly enforced!

It's not surprising that in a hearing of the South Carolina legislature, demands by State Representative Anderson himself for a Sunday law to improve the state of society brought uproarious applause. Who can wonder that the United States president has revealed his willingness to support legislation which would help collapse the separation of church and state!

"...And he spake as a dragon. And he exerciseth all the power of the first beast before him." Revelation 13:11,12.

We haven't seen anything yet! Be prepared to learn some shocking facts. Here's the big question now - who's the first beast?

The
Beast   2
Identified

"**And** I stood upon the sand of the sea, and saw a beast rise up out of the sea, having seven heads and ten horns, and upon his horns ten crowns, and upon his heads the name of blasphemy." Revelation 13:1.

Here is the beast that has the dreaded mark. This mark we definitely don't want! The most awful warning of all time is directed against it {see Rev. 14:9,10}. But before we learn what the mark is, we must discover who the beast is. And it won't be hard. In fact, the Bible makes it so clear that I'll simply list the characteristics of it and you'll be able to tell me who it is! Are you ready? Here we go -

1} A "beast" in prophecy represents a kingdom, a nation, a power. The prophetic book of Daniel tells us - "Thus he said, the fourth beast shall be the fourth kingdom upon earth." Daniel 7:23.

2} This beast comes up out of the "sea." When a beast arises from the "sea," it represents a power rising in a highly populated area, amid "peoples, and multitudes, and nations, and tongues." Revelation 17:15. It would have to conquer the existing government.

3} This beast has seven heads and ten horns. A head represents the headquarters of a government. The head of a county is called the "county seat," you remember.

A "horn" represents a king, a ruler. "And the ten horns out of this kingdom are ten kings that shall arise." Daniel 7:24. The beast is a power with a man at the head of it. You'll find that the Bible explains itself!

4} The beast has "the name of blasphemy" {Rev. 13:1}. What is blasphemy?

Again the Bible gives its own definition. In John 10:32,33, it tells how the Jews were going to stone Jesus. He asked them why they were about to stone Him and they said, "For a good work we stone thee not; but for blasphemy; and because that thou, being a man, makest thyself God."

Amazing! Blasphemy is for a man to claim to be God! Of course Jesus didn't blaspheme because He is God. But for someone less than God - it would be. But there's more.

In Mark 2:3-11, it tells the story of how a paralyzed man wanted to come into a house where Jesus was, but it was just too crowded. He finally persuaded his friends to carry him up on the roof of Peter's house and break it up so they could let the man down into the room where the Saviour was teaching.

Down he comes.

Jesus looks into those pleading eyes and knows that the poor man needs to have forgiveness and peace with God even more than physical healing. Jesus says to him, "Son, thy sins be forgiven thee." Mark 2:5.

Can you imagine the wonderful peace and joy that flooded his soul? But the religious leaders didn't care a thing about the man's soul. They were just trying to catch some words of Jesus that they could use against Him to have Him put to death. The Bible says that they thought, "Why does this man thus speak blasphemies? Who can forgive sins but God only?" The Saviour knew their thoughts and said, "Why reason ye these things in your hearts?" Then He asked them which is easier to say, "thy sins be forgiven," or to say, "arise and walk?" Jesus healed the man before their eyes, and, to the people's utter amazement, he got up and walked out of the house.

Again, Jesus didn't commit blasphemy by forgiving the man's sins because He is a member of the Godhead and had a perfect right to do just that. To whomever He pleased He could say those sweet words of forgiveness, and the very peace of heaven would flood the soul. He could say, "Go and sin no more," and the guilty, depressed, sad, and empty would rise up with peace of mind. They would begin a new and unselfish life of obedience to God - a happy life of peace and joy!

They could slap Him in the face and press a crown of thorns onto that holy brow; they could beat Him until His back was like raw meat, but they couldn't rob Him of His royal right to forgive the chief of sinners. Wonderful Jesus!

But for anyone less than God to claim to forgive sins - it's blasphemy.

Concerning the beast it says, "...And upon his heads the name of blasphemy." Revelation 13:1. The very leaders of this power would both claim to be God on the earth, and claim to have power to forgive men's sins!

5} "And the dragon gave him his power, and his seat, and great authority." Revelation 13:2.

It's clear that the beast gets its "seat" and "authority" from the dragon. But who's the dragon?

Here it is. "And he laid hold on the dragon, that old serpent, which is the Devil and Satan, and bound him a thousand years." Revelation 20:2. The dragon is Satan. But there's more.

"And there appeared another wonder in heaven; and behold a great red dragon, having seven heads and ten horns, and seven crowns upon his heads. And his tail drew the third part of the stars of heaven, and did cast them to the earth: and the dragon stood before the woman which was ready to be delivered, for to devour her child as soon as it was born. And

10

she brought forth a man child, who was to rule all nations with a rod of iron: and her child was caught up unto God, and to his throne." Revelation 12:3-5.

Some years ago, a man in Chicago claimed that he was the man child! Could he have been?

Hardly.

Revelation 19:15,16 shows us that the "Man Child" is Christ.

So the "dragon" represents not only Satan, but also a kingdom through whom Satan worked to try to kill baby Jesus as soon as He was born. Now what kingdom was it whose king decreed the destruction of the babies in Bethlehem?

Of course! It was King Herod. He was employed by, and a representative of, Rome. So here's another clue. The beast gets its power, seat, and authority from Rome!

It's coming clear. The dragon represents Rome. Rome was the empire used by Satan to try to destroy the Saviour of the world! Now let's take a closer look.

The dragon {Rome} had "ten horns." A horn grows out of the head of an animal. A horn, you remember, is a king. When the Roman empire collapsed, ten divisions resulted. Barbarian tribes hammered at the Roman empire for many years until it fell apart and the ten divisions were ruled by ten kings! They were: the Alemani {Germany}, the Franks {France}, Burgundians {Switzerland}, the Suevi {Portugal}, the Anglo-Saxons {Britain}, the Visigoths {Spain}, the Lombards {Italy}, the Vandals, Ostrogoths, and Heruli. The last three were destroyed by the pope of Rome because they refused to become "Christian." The armies of Emperor Justinian, in cooperation with the pope, thrust the Ostrogoths out of the city of Rome. They have become extinct. In 538 A.D. the pope took possession of the city after the emperor decreed that he should be the head of all the Christian churches. These ten divisions of Rome are the ten horns on the "dragon." {For more detail see Appendix 1}. Now look at this -

11

6} "And all that dwell upon the earth shall worship him, whose names are not written in the book of life of the Lamb slain from the foundation of the world." Revelation 13:8.

This is not only a political power but a religious power as well. It demands worship and gets it.

7} It's a world-wide power. "All the world wondered after the beast." Revelation 13:3.

Maybe you already know who the "beast" is.

Can you think of any world-wide political and religious power with a man at the head of it who claims to be God on earth and to be able to forgive sins? Who received its "seat" and authority from Rome? Of a church government whose leader is "wondered after" by the whole world?

Let me say something now that's very important. You see, the reason why God speaks as strongly against worshiping the "beast" as He does is because He loves the people. He loves all people. Reader, He loves you. He knows that a person can't possibly be happy who follows this power and receives its mark. He knows that ". . . they have no rest day nor night, who worship the beast and his image, and whosoever receiveth the mark of his name." Revelation 14:11. In following this power there's no rest. He loves us so much that He warns us in the strongest language known to man. Listen to this -

"And the third angel followed them, saying with a loud voice; If any man worship the beast and his image, and receive his mark in his forehead, or in his hand, the same shall drink of the wine of the wrath of God, which is poured out without mixture into the cup of his indignation." Revelation 14:9,10. Strong language. Language of love is always strong when it's a question of life and death to the one it loves.

I ask you, what more could He do? God sent His own Son to die a hell death in our place. Not one need experience the awful fate of those who follow the beast and receive its mark. Jesus made a way of escape. He suffered the agony of Gethsemane and the torture of His mock trial where they beat Him until His back was like raw meat. They bowed down in mockery and hit Him in the head with a stick - driving the thorns into His brow and sending blood running down His face. Watch Him stagger on His way to Calvary. The Son of God falls on His face in the dirt. He endures the horror of our sins while His blood runs drop by drop to the foot of the cross. Look at His quivering lips as He cries "My God, My God, why hast Thou forsaken Me?"

There He hangs - like a snake on a pole, writhing in agony, drinking the last drops of the wrath of God against sin. "As Moses lifted up the serpent in the wilderness," Jesus was lifted up - for you. He did it for you! He loves you so much! He took in Himself the horrors and death from sin that you and I deserve. Do you see why our Heavenly Father is so anxious that we not follow the beast or receive its mark? We need not receive that awful penalty. Jesus paid it all - for you and me. When they were pounding the spikes through His tender flesh, and Jesus prayed "Father, forgive them, for they know not what they do" - He was praying for you and me then also. He was praying for you! Will you choose Him now as your personal Saviour from sin and death, and follow Him all the way?

You'll be so happy that you did.

Trusting Him; obeying Him; abiding in His love through prayer and Bible study; total surrender, and a loving, happy relationship - only then will you be safe from worshiping the beast and receiving his "mark" - only then. Soon you'll see why.

In identifying the beast, God is not talking about sincere people who are involved with it "ignorantly." Do you know what I mean? When He identifies it, He is talking about "the system," the leaders who know what they are doing, and deliberately disobey and change the word of God. Do you see? Our God is a tender Father. He only holds accountable those who understand what the Bible commands, and knowingly disobey, or, those who turn away from hearing His word and are "willingly ignorant."

The beast exists now. Many honest Christians who are now involved with it will soon learn the facts about it. They will hear God's call to come out of it. And they will respond. Don't be fooled by thinking that the "beast" is a computer in Europe somewhere. That's only a smoke screen to get people off the track that the Bible points out. God's word makes it so clear that even an honest child can see it. The next point in identifying the beast is amazing.

8} It has characteristics of the four beasts {nations} which existed before it. Watch closely -

"And the beast which I saw was like unto a leopard, and his feet were as the feet of a bear, and his mouth as the mouth of a lion: and the dragon gave him his power, and his seat, and great authority." Revelation 13:2.What nations are these? Again, the Bible tells us. The same four beasts are in Daniel 7. "These great beasts, which are four, are four kings, which shall arise out of the earth." Daniel 7:17. These are the four world empires, ruling consecutively from the time of Daniel down to the time of the fall of Rome. They are Babylon {605 - 538 B.C.}, Medo-Persia {538 - 331 B.C.}, Greece {331 - 168 B.C.}, and Rome {168 B.C. - 476 A.D.}. Now let's get the full description of these in Daniel 7.

"Daniel spake and said, I saw in my vision by night, and, behold, the four winds of the heaven strove upon the great sea. And four great beasts came up from the sea, diverse one from another.

"The first was like a lion, and had eagle's wings: I beheld till the wings thereof were plucked, and it was lifted up from the earth, and made stand upon the feet as a man, and a man's heart was given to it. And behold another beast, a second, like to a bear, and it raised up itself on one side, and it had three ribs in the mouth of it between the teeth of it: and they said thus unto it, Arise, devour much flesh. After this I beheld, and

14

lo another, like a leopard, which had upon the back of it four wings of a fowl; the beast had also four heads; and dominion was given to it. After this I saw in the night visions, and behold a fourth beast, dreadful and terrible, and strong exceedingly; and it had great iron teeth: it devoured and brake in pieces, and stamped the residue with the feet of it: and it was diverse from all the beasts that were before it; and it had ten horns. I considered the horns, and behold, there came up among them another little horn, before whom there were three of the first horns plucked up by the roots: and, behold, in this horn were eyes like the eyes of man, and a mouth speaking great things." Daniel 7:2-8.

What a picture! Here they are, beginning with Daniel's day -

The Lion - Babylon.
The Bear - Medo-Persia.
The Leopard - Greece. The
Terrible Beast - Rome.

Since the beast with the mark has similarities of these four, let's take a close look at them.

Babylon {represented by the two-winged lion} ruled the world when Daniel was alive. In the ruins of the ancient city of Babylon, broken statues of lions with two wings have been seen.

The lion - a fit symbol of Babylon. It was the greatest of all the ancient kingdoms. The two wings tell of the swiftness in which the "golden kingdom" conquered the civilized world of that time. How is the "beast" of Revelation 13 like Babylon?

Ancient Babylon, founded by Nimrod {See Genesis 10} the great-grandson of Noah {more than two thousand years before Christ} was one of the wonders of the world. It was laid out in a perfect square with a great and high wall eighty-seven feet thick. Its two hundred and twenty-five square miles of enclosed surface was laid out in beautiful symmetry and interspersed with luxuriant pleasure grounds and gardens. With its sixty miles of moat, its sixty miles of outer wall, its gates of solid brass, its hanging gardens, its subterranean tunnel under the River Euphrates, its perfect arrangement for beauty and defense - this city, containing in itself many things which were themselves wonders of the world, was itself another and still mightier wonder.[1]

The emperors of Babylon claimed worship as gods. For man to be appreciated is great, but to be worshiped by other humans is blasphemous. The leader of the "beast" does this very thing! What about the next kingdom?

Medo-Persia took over on that terrible night when King Belshazzar, the last king of Babylon, half drunk, threw a party for a thousand of his lords and tossed the sacred vessels from the temple of God about the floor. That was the last straw. His knees knocked together in fear as he watched a bloodless hand trace his doom upon the palace wall. Look at this description of that fearful night.

"Belshazzar the king made a great feast to a thousand of his lords, and drank wine before the thousand. Then they brought the golden vessels that were taken out of the temple of the house of God, which was at Jerusalem; and the king, and his princes, his wives, and his concubines, drank in them. In the same hour came forth fingers of a man's hand, and wrote over against the candlestick upon the plaster of the wall of the king's palace: and the king saw the part of the hand that wrote. Then the king's countenance was changed, and his thoughts troubled him, so that the joints of his loins were loosed, and his knees smote one against another." Daniel 5:1,3,5.

What a scene!

At sight of that bloodless hand, Belshazzar is paralyzed with fear. He calls in all the "astrologers, the Chaldeans, and the soothsayers," but they're no help. Finally, the queen suggests that Daniel be called in. The corrupt king isn't ignorant of the fact that Daniel had shown himself able to interpret dreams and solve mysteries, because the God of heaven was with him. But Belshazzar hates God and doesn't even class Daniel with the wise men.

But now! Now he's scared to death. At the queen's suggestion Daniel is called in. Watch what happens -

"Then was Daniel brought in before the king. And the king spake and said unto Daniel, Art thou Daniel, which art of the children of the captivity of Judah, whom the king my father brought out of Jewry?" Daniel 5:13.

After mentioning the failure of his magicians to read the writing on the wall, the king said, "And I have heard of thee, that thou canst make interpretations, and dissolve doubts: now if thou canst read the writing, and make known to me the interpretation thereof, thou shalt be clothed with scarlet, and have a chain of gold about thy neck, and shalt be the third ruler in the kingdom." Daniel 5:16

Daniel well knew what would happen that night, and earth-ly rewards sank into nothingness. In a few hours most in that court would be dead. He had no heart for rewards.

"Let thy gifts," he said, "be to thyself and give thy rewards to another; yet I will read the writing unto the king, and make known to him the interpretation." Daniel 5:17.

After reminding the king of his rebellion and pride against God, he told him what the writing meant. Now came the shocking news.

"And this," Daniel declared, "is the writing that was written, MENE, MENE, TEKEL, UPHARSIN. This is the interpretation of the thing: MENE: God hath numbered thy kingdom, and finished it, TEKEL: Thou art weighed in the balances, and art found wanting. PERES: Thy kingdom is divided, and given to the Medes and Persians." Daniel 5:25-28. The king is stunned. Can you imagine the desperation! He didn't have long to be in suspense.

"In that night was Belshazzar the king of the Chaldeans slain. And Darius the Median took the kingdom, being about three score and two years old." Daniel 5:30,31. "Crownless and scepterless, Belshazzar lay - a robe of purple 'round a form of clay'."

There we have it. The two-winged lion was dead. The year - 538 B.C. Medo- Persia under Darius had taken over right on schedule! The bear of Daniel's dream had conquered the world!

How is the "beast" of Revelation 13 like Medo-Persia?

The Medo-Persians had a rule that once they made a law - it stuck, and could never be reversed. The government was considered infallible.

You'll see shortly that the "beast" power takes this same policy.

Medo-Persia ruled until the empire met up with a young man whose military genius was uncanny - Alexander the Great.

He became a great ruler at the age of 25!

It was October 1, 331 B.C. At the head of his armies Alexander met the Persian forces head on and defeated them in the battle of Arbela. His military genius made Greece to emerge as the third world empire.

The leopard with four heads and four wings of Daniel's vision had replaced the Medo-Persian bear.

But why the four heads?

Alexander had conquered the world. But he hadn't conquered himself. At a drunken debauch he drank the Herculean cup full of alcohol. It was a huge thing. The human stomach can hardly hold more than a quart.

Of all horrors. He drank it twice! And it killed him. Alexander died with a raging fever at the age of 33. The year - 323 B.C.

His will had declared that the kingdom should go "to the strongest." His four generals, Cassander, Lysimachus, Seleuchus and Ptolomy took over the empire and divided it into four parts. These divisions are represented by the four

18

heads of the leopard beast.

What about the four wings? They represent swiftness. Greece had conquered the world in only 13 years. Such a feat has never been equaled.

{For more information on the four divisions of Greece, see Funk and Wagnell's New Encyclopedia on "Alexander III," pg. 390, 391}.

Before his death, Alexander had ordered the Greek cities to worship him as a god. The "beast" of Revelation 13 is "like unto a leopard" because it took on the Greek culture and also has a leader that claims worship as God.

Who is the fourth "terrible" beast of Daniel 7?

"After this I saw in the night visions, and behold a fourth beast, dreadful and terrible, and strong exceedingly; and it had great iron teeth: it devoured and brake in pieces, and stamped the residue with the feet of it: . . . and it had ten horns." "The fourth beast shall be the fourth kingdom upon earth." Daniel 7:7, 23.

The fourth kingdom, represented by this terrible beast is Rome. Rome conquered Greece in 168 B.C. and eventually gave its power to the "beast" of Revelation 13. Out of the fourth "terrible beast" comes a "little horn."

Now here's something amazing. The beast of Revelation 13, and the "little horn" of Daniel 7, are one and the same power! God wants to make sure that there's no mistaking who this power is, so He describes it in both prophetic books.

Isn't Bible prophecy fantastic! Look at the description of the "little horn."

"I considered the horns, and behold, there came up among them another little horn, before whom there were three of the first horns plucked up by the roots: and, behold, in this horn were eyes like the eyes of man, and a mouth speaking great things. . . And he shall subdue three kings. And he shall speak great words against the most High, and think to change times and laws; and they shall be given into his hand until a time and times and the dividing of time." Daniel 7:8, 24, 25.

If you compare this description of the "little horn" with the description of the "beast" of Revelation 13, you'll see that they are one and the same power. (For the amazing comparison, see Appendix 1A).

One of the most startling things about this power is that it would "think to change times and laws." Daniel 7:25. Here's a man that sets himself up as equal with God, and dares to tamper with His law - the constitution of the universe! With blasphemous audacity he does his work. But God has said, "All His commandments are sure. They stand fast forever and ever." Psalms 111:7, 8.

The next clue to identify the beast, is the time period which God gives for its reign before it receives its "deadly wound." It would reign for 1260 years. Just so there's no mistake on this, He repeats this period seven times in Daniel and Revelation! {For a detailed description of this fantastic time prophecy, see Appendix 2.}

Now - just one more clue before I tell you who the beast is.

It's not only the same as the "little horn" of Daniel 7, but it's also the same power as the great whore riding upon the scarlet colored beast of Revelation 17. Let's take a shocking glimpse.

"And there came one of the seven angels which had the seven vials, and talked with me, saying unto me, Come hither; I will shew unto thee the judgment of the great whore that sitteth upon many waters: . . . and I saw a woman sit upon a scarlet coloured beast, full of names of blasphemy, having seven heads and ten horns." Revelation 17:1-3.

There are those heads and horns again. We've come to associate them with Rome. The Harlot is controlling Rome - riding it around - making her seat on it. Familiar isn't it! Now it gets even clearer.

This "harlot" represents a corrupt church system. And get this - "And the woman was arrayed in purple and scarlet colour, and decked with gold and precious stones and pearls." Revelation 17:4. It's a rich church.

A woman in Bible prophecy represents a church. God likens His people to a "comely and delicate woman." Jeremiah 6:2. A virgin is God's pure church. A harlot {whore} is a corrupt church.

Right here in verse 5 she's called "THE MOTHER OF HARLOTS AND ABOMINATIONS OF THE EARTH." Revelation 17:5. It's not only a church, it's a mother church. It's a world power. But get this -

"And I saw the woman drunken with the blood of the saints, and with the blood of the martyrs of Jesus: and when I saw her I wondered with great admiration." Revelation 17:6. Oh yes! It kills God's people!

Amazing! Why would our heavenly Father Who is so loving and kind talk this way about a church, of all things, and expose it to the world? Why does He Who is so full of pity and love warn anyone who even follows this power and receives its mark that they will end up in the lake of fire?

The answer is - because it's true. Though God is very tenderhearted, He always tells the truth.

I know it's shocking, but here's a corrupt church power that Satan has used to deceive the whole world and rob men and women of their eternal life by using deception. Like Nimrod and Alexander the Great, this power has leaders who divert the attention and worship of the people from the true, living God, to themselves. These leaders turn people from heeding the word of God to heeding their word; from obeying the commandments of God, to obeying their commandments. This is why God tells it like it is - because He is love.

And remember, there are many sincere, lovely Christians in this fallen church, named "Babylon," and they will hear God's call and come out.

Look at this! "And he cried mightily with a strong voice, saying, Babylon the great is fallen, is fallen, and is become the habitation of devils, and the hold of every foul spirit, and a cage of every unclean and hateful bird."

"And I heard another voice from heaven, saying, Come out of her, my people, that ye be not partakers of her sins, and that ye receive not of her plagues. For her sins have reached unto heaven, and God hath remembered her iniquities." Revelation 18:2, 4, 5. Amazing!

Now - who is this "beast?" What power -

1} - Received its "seat" and authority from Rome. Revelation 13:4.

2} - Rules the world for 1260 years {from 538 A.D. - 1798 A.D.}.

3} - Then received a "deadly wound" which later heals. Revelation 13:3.

4} - Is both a political and a religious power, which is worshiped. Revelation 13:4.

5} - Tampered with God's law. Daniel 7:25.

6} - Has a leader who claims to be God on the earth and to be able to forgive sins {blasphemy}. Revelation 13:1.

7} - Is a mother church {daughters have come out of her}. Revelation 17:5.

8} - Made war with the saints. Revelation 13:7.

9} - Is a world power which is wondered at. Revelation 13:3, 4.

10} - Has "a man" at the head of it with the number of his name being 666. Revelation 13:18.

11} - Has a dreaded "mark" which will cause you, or any person, to be cast into the lake of fire and lose eternal life. Revelation 14:9, 10.

By now, most of the people have guessed that it's the Papacy. They're correct. It's the only power on the face of the earth that fits all the Bible characteristics for it.

But what about **666?**

The *BEAST* Described 3

STOP! If you haven't read chapter 2, "The Beast Identified," don't read this chapter.

Let's take a close look at this thing to make sure there's no mistake.

"And the dragon gave him his power, and his seat, and great authority." Revelation 13:2.

Emperor Justinian "gave" the power of Rome to the pope when he decreed that the pope should be over all the Christian churches of the earth. The Papacy was established in 538 A.D., when the Emperor's general Belisarius drove the Ostrogoths from Rome.

Rome gave him his "seat." Bible prophecy predicted it hundreds of years before it happened!

From 538 A.D. the Papacy ruled for exactly 1260 years, until 1798 when something incredible happened. The pope was taken prisoner! Napoleon's general, Berthier, captured the pope and took him to France! He later died.

A deadly wound. The Papacy had reigned exactly 1260 years. Could it have just been coincidence? Why did Berthier do it?

Napoleon wanted to rule the world. The Papacy stood in his way. I wonder if they knew that they were fulfilling prophecy in spite of themselves!

"... And his deadly wound was healed; and all the world wondered after the beast." Revelation 13:3.

23

"In 1929, the Italian government recognized Vatican City as an independent state. Once again, the pope was king. On March 9, 1929, he said, "The peoples of the entire world are with us." The San Francisco Chronicle published an account of the pact signing on the front page of its newspaper. It actually read like this, "Mussolini and Gaspari Sign Historic Pact... Heal Wound of Many Years." That's fantastic! The Bible predicted that its wound would be healed, and the newspaper confirmed it in the exact same words.[1]

Though this great organization was not officially established until 538 A.D., the apostle Paul saw forces at work that were preparing the way. What was going on back there that he could have seen? Here's what happened.

After Jesus went back to heaven, the early church grew rapidly under the blessing of the Holy Spirit. Jesus had predicted the treatment that His people were to receive.

"Then shall they deliver you up to be afflicted, and shall kill you; and ye shall be hated of all nations for my name's sake." Matthew 24:9. That was literally fulfilled. Look at this amazing account -

"Their execution was made into a game," wrote Tacitus, describing the persecutions under Nero. "They were covered with the skins of wild animals and torn to pieces by dogs. They were hung on crosses. They were burned, wrapped in flammable material and set on fire, to illuminate the night.

"To escape death, they had but to repudiate Christ and sacrifice to the emperor." Some did, but many more were tortured to death rather than deny their Lord.

"Paganism foresaw that should the gospel triumph, her temples and altars would be swept away; therefore she summoned her forces to destroy Christianity. Christians were stripped of their possessions and driven from their homes. Great numbers sealed their testimony with their blood. Noble and slave, rich and poor, learned and ignorant, were alike slain without mercy.

"Beneath the hills outside the city of Rome, long galleries had been tunneled through earth and rock; the dark and intricate network of passages extended for miles beyond the city walls. In these underground retreats the followers of

Christ buried their dead; and here also, when suspected, they found a home. Many were 'tortured, not accepting deliverance; that they might obtain a better resurrection.' Hebrews 11:35 They rejoiced that they were accounted worthy to suffer for the truth, and songs of triumph ascended from the midst of the crackling flames."[2]

Satan couldn't wipe them out. For years, Emperors Nero and Diocletian slaughtered them by the thousands.

"You may kill us, torture us, condemn us," said one Christian to his persecutors, "your injustice is the proof that we are innocent." Tertullian, Apology, para. 50.

Until 313 A.D. it was against the law to be a Christian. Such a person was an automatic criminal. But the followers of Jesus spread everywhere.

Satan could see that he had to change his tactics. He would come up with a better scheme. What could the devil think of to do that would be better than killing Christians?

Make things easy - and infiltrate! Like a wise general he would corrupt the church from the inside!

Watch what happens.

A great shout goes up in the empire. Emperor Constantine has become a Christian! The Christians are euphoric.

No more being torn apart by dogs and lions, or used as dupes to be cut down in cold blood, or human torches to light up the arena for the gladiators. Now Christianity is the state religion! Things are going great. Or so it seems.

But little by little, as everyone relaxes and quits worrying about being tortured to death, something happens. Compromise!

Gradually the leaders, for the sake of popularity and gain, let down the standards to make it easier for the pagans to come into the church. But this brings in errors and pagan customs.

Not at all surprised by Satan's scheme to corrupt His church from within, God gives us fair warning. Listen to Paul's shocking words.

"Let no man deceive you by any means: for that day [of the Lord] shall not come, except there come a falling away

25

first, and that man of sin be revealed, the son of perdition; who opposeth and exalteth himself above all that is called God, or that is worshipped; so that he as God sitteth in the temple of God, shewing himself that he is God." "For the mystery of iniquity doth already work:" II Thessalonians 2:1, 2, 3, 4, 7.

Oh yes! He saw it coming. The mysterious work of corruption rapidly progressed after the death of the last apostle.

Question: What happened?

After persecution ceased, Satan's great device was to control the leaders of the church. If he could inflate their ego, make them money hungry, the whole body would be affected. A popularity contest would be on to get as many heathen to accept Christianity as possible. The wealth and prestige of the church would grow. Who cares if you have to change the Bible somewhat to get them! Just introduce some of the heathen customs and rites into Christianity, give them Christian names, and the heathen will flock in.

Of all horrors - that's just what happened!

The apostles had gone throughout the empire establishing churches in many cities. As time went by, smaller churches were built in the surrounding countrysides. The large centers were in Jerusalem, Rome, and Alexandria, Egypt. Rome finally emerged on top.

The next step in the plot was for church leaders to get control of the state, to help enforce their decrees. They achieved this beyond their wildest dreams. The epitome of this came when in 538 A.D. the entire city of Rome was handed over to the pope - the Bishop of Rome. For the next 1260 years, church leaders reigned with full civil authority. All just as predicted in prophecy!

Incredible!

But look at this shocker.

It says that the beast has "the name of blasphemy." Revelation 13:1. It became one of the leading doctrines of the church that its visible head is invested with supreme authority over bishops and pastors in all parts of the world. More than this, he took the very name of God! He was addressed as "Lord God the Pope" and declared to be "infallible." (For documentation on this, see Appendix 3). He demands the worship of all men.

What about 666? Let's take a shocking look.

On the pope's official mitre has been seen the title "Vicarius Filii Dei," which means "Vicar of the Son of God."

The claim that this is his official title has been stated publicly through the years. The April 18, 1915 issue of <u>Our Sunday Visitor</u> states: "The letters inscribed in the pope's mitre are these: 'VICARIUS FILII DEI,' which is Latin for Vicar of the Son of God."

In Revelation 13:18 it says, "Count the number of the beast; for it is the number of a man; and his number is Six hundred threescore and six (666)."

Let's do it now and see what we find. Remember the Roman numerals you learned in school?

V = 5
I = 1
C = 100
A = 0
R = 0
I = 1
U = 5
S = 0
F = 0
I = 1
L = 50
I = 1
I = 1

D = 500
E = 0
I = 1
_____

  Total = 666 !!!

"U" and "V" have the same value. Look in your encyclopedia under "alphabet."

One example is that on the "Arch of Titus" in Rome, it says, "Titvs" using a "v" for a "u."

27

I want to be quick to say that when a person shares this shocking revelation, he must be kind and tactful. We must let people know that God loves all. The truth must be told - but always in kindness.

The 1260 years of the Papacy's rule are called the "dark ages." I'm sure you've heard that expression before. The reason it was so dark is because the priests forbade anyone to read or even have a Bible! For hundreds of years only the priests were allowed to read Bibles. Satan had to get the Bibles away from the people in order to keep them in darkness and superstition. The people just didn't know any better. There was a time when if you were caught with a Bible, you were dragged out of your home, hung up on a pole, and burned alive in your front yard! (For documentation, see Appendix 4).

What John sees next is so unbelievable that he's stunned.

Dynamite   *4*

STOP! IF YOU HAVEN'T READ CHAPTER 2, "THE BEAST IDENTIFIED," DON'T READ THIS CHAPTER.

Can you imagine Christians killing other Christians? A horrible thought!

Get this, "And it was given unto him to make war with the saints, and to overcome them." Revelation 13:7. "And I saw the woman drunken with the blood of the saints, and with the blood of the martyrs of Jesus: and when I saw her I wondered with great admiration." Revelation 17:6.

What a picture! No wonder John was so amazed. A stack of books could hardly contain the accounts of the 50 million Christians put to death as "heretics." For possessing a Bible, for believing that people ought to be free to worship God according to their own conscience, for these and many other "crimes," men, women, and little children were tortured to death.

History comes through loud and clear that whole villages and towns were wiped off the map for not conforming to the state church and her leader.

"Dignitaries of the church studied, under Satan their master, to invent means to cause the greatest possible torture and not end the life of the victim. In many cases the infernal process was repeated to the utmost limit of human endurance, until nature gave up the struggle, and the sufferer hailed death as a sweet release."[1] Such was the fate of those who opposed the church of Rome. If given opportunity in the U.S., she would do the same today against "heretics." Her boast is that she never changes. The rector of the Catholic Institute of Paris, H.M.A. Baudrillart, revealed the attitude of the church and her leaders toward persecution. Watch closely -

"When confronted with heresy," he said, "she does not content herself with persuasion, arguments of an intellectual and moral order appear to her insufficient, and she has recourse to force, to corporal punishment, to torture."[2]

For a shocking account of how the Waldenses, Albigenses, Bohemians, and others were massacred, or slowly and secretly murdered for their faith, see Appendix 5.

The most outstanding story is the one of the Waldenses. They were some of the few people who had copies of the Bible during the early years of the Papacy's reign.

They saw that under the guidance of Pope and priest, multitudes were vainly endeavoring to obtain pardon by afflicting their bodies for the sin of their souls. Oppressed with a sense of sin, and haunted with the fear of God's avenging wrath, many suffered on, until exhausted nature gave way and without one ray of light or hope they sank into the tomb.

The Waldenses longed to break to these starving souls the bread of life, to open to them the messages of peace in the promises of God, and to point them to Christ as the only hope of salvation.

The Saviour was represented by the priests as so devoid of sympathy with man in his fallen state that the mediation of priests and saints must be invoked. The Waldenses longed to point these souls to Jesus as their compassionate, loving Saviour, standing with outstretched arms, inviting all to come to Him with their burden of sin, and obtain pardon and peace.

With quivering lip and tearful eye did he, often on bended knees, open to others the precious promises that reveal the sinner's only hope. Especially was the repetition of these

30

words eagerly desired: "The blood of Jesus Christ His Son cleanseth us from all sin." I John 1:7.

Many were undeceived in regard to the claims of Rome. They saw how vain is the mediation of men in behalf of the sinner.

The assurance of a Saviour's love seemed too much for some of these poor, tempest tossed souls to realize. So great was the relief which it brought, such a flood of light was shed upon them, that they seemed transported to heaven. Often would words like these be uttered: "Will God indeed accept my offering? Will He smile upon me? Will He pardon me?" The answer was read: "Come unto Me, all ye that labor and are heavy laden, and I will give you rest." Matthew 11:28.

Faith grasped the promise, and the glad response was heard: "No more long pilgrimages to make; no more painful journeys to holy shrines. I may come to Jesus just as I am, and He will not spurn my prayer. 'Thy sins be forgiven thee.' Mine, even mine, may be forgiven!" [Praise God!]

There was a strange and solemn power in the words of Scripture that spoke directly to the hearts of those who were longing for the truth. It was the voice of God, and it carried conviction to those who heard.

In many cases the messenger of truth was seen no more. He had made his way to other lands, or he was wearing out his life in some unknown dungeon, or perhaps his bones were whitening on the spot where he had witnessed for the truth.

The Waldensian missionaries were invading the kingdom of Satan. The very existence of this people, holding the faith of the ancient church, was a constant testimony to Rome's apostasy, and excited the most bitter hatred and persecution. Their refusal to surrender the Scriptures was an offense that Rome could not tolerate. She determined to blot them from the earth.

Pope Innocent VIII ordered "That malicious and abominable sect of malignants," if they "refuse to abjure, to be crushed like venomous snakes."!! (See Appendix 6).

No charge could be brought against their moral character. Their grand offense was that they would not worship God according to the will of the pope. For this crime, every disgrace, insult, and torture that men or devils could invent was heaped upon them.

They were hunted to death; yet their blood watered the seed sown, and it failed not of yielding fruit. Scattered over many lands ... it will be carried forward to the close of time by those who also are willing to suffer all things "for the word of God, and for the testimony of Jesus Christ." Revelation 1:9.[3]

Keep in mind that these atrocities happened long before we were born. But the warning against receiving the "mark of the beast" is certainly for us today. Soon, you'll know what the beast's "mark" is!

As we've learned, this power would "think to change times and laws." Daniel 7:25.

How could it possibly do that?

Since the heathen were used to worshiping images, the church ripped out the second commandment which forbids image worship. They placed images in the churches! But instead of images of heathen gods, they simply used images of dead Christians! The people were taught that these were merely to help increase their learning and devotion. But the result was far different.

For documentation on how images were brought into the churches, see Appendix 7.

It says that he would "think to change times and laws." Look at this shocking statement from an official decretal -

"The Pope has power to change times, to abrogate (change) laws, and to dispense with all things, even the precepts of Christ." Decretal, de Tranlatic Episcop.

Unbelievable!

It makes your mouth fall open. I was amazed that the official statement of the Papacy was nearly a word for word quote from the Bible! Instead of leaving only nine commandments, they cut the tenth one in two, so there would still be ten. (See Appendix 8)

Satan had caused the second commandment to be ripped out. But he wasn't finished. The leaders changed the fourth one also!

The change of the fourth commandment was attempted gradually over a period of time so as not to arouse anyone. But the change is a masterpiece of Satan's work. Get ready for a shock. The following mind-boggling statements were made by church authorities and are documented -

"Question - Have you any other way of proving that the church (Roman Catholic) has power to institute festivals of precept?

"Answer - Had she not such power, she could not have done that in which all modern religionists agree with her - she could not have substituted the observance of Sunday, the first day of the week, for the observance of Saturday, the seventh day, a change for which there is no scriptural authority." *A Doctrinal Catechism*, by Stephen Keenan, pg. 174.

Incredible!

"The Catholic Church," declared Cardinal Gibbons, "by virtue of her divine mission changed the day from Saturday to Sunday."[4]

Again the question is asked to them:

"Question - Which is the Sabbath day?

"Answer - Saturday is the Sabbath day.

"Question - Why do we observe Sunday instead of Saturday?

"Answer - We observe Sunday instead of Saturday because the Catholic Church, in the Council of Laodicea (A.D. 364), transferred the solemnity from Saturday to Sunday." *The Convert's Catechism of Catholic Doctrine,* pg. 50, third edition.

What does the fourth commandment actually say? Here it is:

"Remember the Sabbath day, to keep it holy. Six days shalt thou labour, and do all thy work: But the seventh day is the Sabbath of the Lord thy God: in it thou shalt not do any work, thou, nor thy son, nor thy daughter, thy manservant, nor thy maidservant, nor thy cattle, nor thy stranger that is within thy gates: For in six days the Lord made heaven and earth, the sea, and all that in them is, and rested the seventh day: wherefore the Lord blessed the Sabbath day, and hallowed it." Exodus 20:8-11.

Do church authorities acknowledge that there is no command in the Bible for the sanctification of Sunday?

They do! Look at this -

Catholic Cardinal Gibbons, in *Faith of Our Fathers,* pg. 111, said, "You may read the Bible from Genesis to Revelation, and you will not find a single line authorizing the sanctification of Sunday. The Scriptures enforce the religious observance of Saturday, a day which we never sanctify."

Amazing! You see, in the Council of Trent (1545 A.D.), church leaders ruled that "tradition" is of as great authority as the Bible! They believed that God had given them the authority to change the Bible any way they pleased. By "tradition" they meant human teachings.

Jesus said, "But in vain they do worship me, teaching for doctrines the commandments of men." Matthew 15:9.

Just as they had brought images into the church to make it easier for the pagans to come in, they changed the Sabbath of the Bible for the same reason.

How did it all start?

The sun was the main god of the heathen even back as far as ancient Babylon. Since they worshiped the sun on Sunday, the compromising church leaders could see that if they changed the Sabbath from Saturday to Sunday, it would accomplish several things.

1) - It would separate them from the Jews who were hated by many of the Romans and who, along with Jesus, (Luke

34

4:16), had been worshiping on Saturday from the beginning (and still do today).

2) - It would make it much easier for the pagans to come into the church if the Christians met on the same day that the pagan world did.

It worked well. Pagans flocked in by the thousands. Satan's plan of compromise was doing its baleful work. The change was attempted gradually, but many of the true hearted, loyal Christians were alarmed. They came to the leaders and wanted to know why they had dared tamper with the law of Almighty God! The church leaders knew this would happen - and they had an answer ready. It's a masterpiece. If a person doesn't know the Bible well it sounds good.

The people were told that they were worshiping on Sunday now because Jesus rose from the dead on that day.

There's not even one verse in the Bible that tells us to do this, but that's what they were told. Amazing! Maybe you've even heard it yourself! Many don't realize it, but in Romans 6:3-5 we see that it's baptism that represents the resurrection {coming up out of the water} to a new life in Christ – not the day of the sun.

When Emperor Constantine became a Christian, Christianity became the state religion, you remember. As thousands of sun-worshipers flocked into the church, it wasn't long before they had a dominating influence. Most of his top officials had been sun-worshipers. Because the Roman government was getting shaky, Constantine consulted with his aides and with the church officials in Rome.

"What shall we do? How can we unite and stabilize the government?" The counsel of the church leaders was timely -

"Pass a Sunday law. Force everyone to cease work and honor Sunday."

That was it! It would satisfy the sun-worshiping pagans, and unite pagans, Christians, and the Roman empire as never before!

35

The year is 321 A.D. Constantine, yielding to the suggestion of church leaders, passes the first Sunday law! Here it is, straight out of the record:

"Let all the judges and town people, and the occupation of all trades rest on the venerable day of the sun." Edict of March 7, 321 A.D. Corpus Juris Civilis Cod., lib. 3, tit. 12, Lex. 3. (For more information on this, see Appendix 9).

The Christians who would not compromise and dishonor God found themselves in a dilemma. Satan had worked things around so that you were forced to honor the pagan "day of the sun" or pay the penalty. Even after the Emperor's Sunday law, many Christians continued to honor and keep holy the seventh-day Sabbath that their Saviour had kept. God knew what was going on and had predicted that the man of sin would "think to change times and laws." Satan was about to pull off a world-wide hoax.

Bibles were forbidden by the priests. As the years went by, the new generations (without Bibles) would forget all about the Sabbath of the Lord.

Not only that - from time to time, great church councils were held. In nearly every one, the Sabbath which God had given as a memorial of His creation of the world was pressed down, and Sunday was exalted. The pagan festival of Sunday finally came to be regarded as the "Lord's day" (by Pope Sylvester, 314-337 A.D.) and the church leaders pronounced the Bible Sabbath a relic of the Jews, and those who honored it, {in obedience to the fourth commandment of God} were pronounced to be "accursed."

To rip out the commandment right in the center, put in Sunday worship as a counterfeit, take the Bibles away, and command the whole world to accept it - this was the king of all swindles!

You see, Satan hates the fourth commandment more than all others because it is the only one that tells who God really is - the Creator of "Heaven and earth, the sea, and all that in

36

them is." Exodus 20:11. You could worship any god and keep the other nine (not kill, steal, etc.) but to keep the fourth commandment you must worship the Creator of the Universe Who Himself rested on the seventh day and commanded His people to do the same in a love relationship with Himself.

As the centuries went by, the people, with no Bibles, forgot about God's Sabbath, and Sunday worship became firmly established. Many even today are ignorant on the subject.

The Waldenses, which I have mentioned, and some other groups through the dark ages did secretly have Bibles, and many did keep the Bible Sabbath on Saturday like Jesus did - all down through history. But they were treated as outlaws. Whenever they were caught they were tortured to death. Their mangled corpses show the world the tactics that the beast has always used - force.

Of God's faithful in the last days it says, "Here is the patience of the saints; here are they that keep the commandments of God, and the faith of Jesus." Revelation 14:12.

In modern times, leaders who know what they are talking about will admit that men changed the Sabbath and not God. Look at these startling statements from Protestant leaders:

Methodist - "The reason we observe the first day instead of the seventh is based on no positive command. One will search the Scriptures in vain for authority for changing from the seventh day to the first." Clovis G. Chappell, *Ten Rules For Living,* pg. 61.

Baptist - Harold Lindsell, former editor of Christianity Today, said, "There is nothing in Scripture that requires us to keep Sunday rather than Saturday as a holy day." Christianity Today, November 5, 1976.

Episcopal - "The Bible commandment says on the seventh day thou shalt rest. That is Saturday. Nowhere in the Bible is it laid down that worship should be done on Sunday." Philip Carrington, Toronto Daily Star, October 26, 1949.

37

Our Catholic friends know how the change came about. They say, "We observe Sunday instead of Saturday because the Catholic Church in the Council of Laodicea, transferred the solemnity from Saturday to Sunday." *The Convert's Catechism of Catholic Doctrine,* Third edition, pg. 50.

The Catholic Press said, "Sunday is a Catholic institution, and its claims to observation can be defended only on Catholic principles . . . From beginning to end of Scripture there is not a single passage that warrants the transfer of weekly public worship from the last day of the week to the first."[5]

God speaks of the seventh day 126 times in the Old Testament and 62 times in the New. The first day of the week is mentioned only eight times in the New Testament. A Catholic priest offered $1000 to anyone who could find one Bible verse to indicate that Sunday is now holy and should be observed instead of the seventh day. No one responded. I have done the same, but received no response. Why not?

For an amazing glimpse of the eight Bible texts which mention the first day of the week, see Appendix 10.

It says that the beast (little horn power) would "think to change times and laws." Daniel 7:25.

The second commandment was ripped out and images were brought in. The fourth commandment is the only one that deals with time. Look at this shocking announcement:

"The Pope has power to change times, to abrogate laws, and to dispense with all things, even the precepts of Christ. . . . The Pope has authority, and has often exercised it, to dispense with the command of Christ." Decretal, de Tranlatic Episcop. Cap.

Keep in mind that our God is kind and fair. Those who are keeping Sunday and breaking God's fourth commandment ignorantly are not under condemnation. Don't forget that. It's only those who know what God commands and willfully disobey who are committing sin. God's enemy knows that to break one of God's commandments is a sin which hurts our

Saviour and robs us of eternal life with Him if not repented of.

Satan laid this plot so deep that even many ministers are not aware of it. Many religious leaders are putting forth desperate efforts to keep the facts on this subject away from the people. Shocking but true, many ministers have not learned at school anything different than their teachers have learned before them. Then they teach their congregations what they learned from their teachers. It is perpetuated for generations. This is why even your own parents or grandparents may not have understood what God's word teaches about His seventh-day Sabbath. But when people honestly study the Bible for themselves - their eyes are opened. Praise God! Many take their preacher's word and just don't study God's word for themselves. Do you believe that?

I praise God that many millions of people around the world are learning these amazing truths about God's true Sabbath of the Bible and are starting to keep it holy in loving obedience to the Saviour Who died to redeem them.

As you begin to keep God's Sabbath holy, it becomes a delight. Sweet peace and joy fill your heart. You know that now you're not violating any of His loving commands but are walking more closely with the Saviour. Revelation describes the faithful in the last days who "keep the commandments of God and the faith of Jesus." Revelation 14:12.

The devil has been trying to get preachers to say that God's ten commandments have been done away with. But when will it ever be right to break God's sixth, eighth, or ninth commandments to kill, steal or lie? All ten stand or fall together because it's a sweet love relationship between you and God. In James 2:10,11 God says that if you break one, you break them all. It's like two lovers - it's either all or nothing.

The lovely Jesus said, "Think not that I am come to destroy the law or the prophets: I am not come to destroy, but to fulfill. For verily I say unto you, Till heaven and earth pass, one jot or one tittle shall in no wise pass from the law, till all be fulfilled." Matthew 5:17,18. Heaven and earth haven't passed away yet!

We are saved by God's free grace and not by our obedience (Ephesians 2:8). His salvation is a free gift which we can receive by simple faith. But it's also true that if a person willfully, persistently disobeys God, it shows that he really doesn't love God enough to obey Him, and hasn't received this free gift. He hasn't been born again. God's true people will be obedient, happy people who love Him so much that they would rather die than sin against Him any more! Obedience becomes a joy when you're walking with Jesus!

It's new to many people that Moses received more than one set of laws. On one trip up the mountain, God gave him the ten commandments which He says will stand forever. At another time, Moses received the ceremonial law which is discussed in Appendix 11. This law regulated the killing of animals. It was "added because of sin" and pointed forward to the sacrifice of the Son of God on the cross. It was to keep fresh in the people's minds that some day the real sacrifice for sin would come. The innocent little lamb represented "The Lamb of God which taketh away the sin of the world." John 1:29. Since Jesus really came and died for us, it's easy to see that God doesn't require us to kill animals any more. Aren't you glad?

There was another set of laws that God gave to His people. They were the health laws as found in Leviticus 11, and Deuteronomy 14. Because of these, God's people were the healthiest people in the world! They didn't get the horrible diseases of the other nations, or even like we have in ourworld today. Since our stomachs and bodies are the same as theirs, those who follow these wise, and scientific health laws today also reap the delightful benefits. They just don't get the terrifying cancer, heart attack, etc. like others. Our God is so kind! It makes you fall in love with that lovely Person - Jesus.

It was the ceremonial law of Moses that was done away with on the cross. This law had animal sacrifices, meat and drink offerings, and seven ceremonial sabbaths that rotated through the year and fell on various days of the week.

The ceremonial law pointed forward to the death of dear Jesus on the cross, and is not required of us now. These ceremonial meat and drink offerings, new moons and sabbath days were a "shadow of things to come; but the body is of Christ." Colossians 2:16,17. They were all a "shadow" of the cross. Paul calls it the "handwriting of ordinances" and makes it clear that it was nailed to "His cross." Colossians 2:14.

The seven ceremonial sabbaths that rotated through the year are not required of us now, and were totally separate from the "Sabbath of the Lord" that came every week. Not only does God want His people to observe His weekly Sabbath here on earth in a happy relationship with Himself, but the Bible says that we will still be keeping it even in heaven! Isaiah 66:22,23. For the eye-opening documentation showing the difference between the ceremonial law and the ten commandments, see Appendix 11.

Satan has palmed off the biggest counterfeit in the history of man!

Look at this shocker - The Catholic authorities proclaim: "The Bible says, 'Remember that thou keep holy the Sabbath day.' The Catholic Church says, No! By my divine power I abolish the Sabbath day, and command you to keep the first day of the week. And lo, the entire civilized world bows down in reverent obedience to the command of the holy Catholic Church!" Father Enright, C.S.S.R. of the Redemptoral College, Kansas City, Mo., as taken from *History of the Sabbath*, pg. 802.

Amazing! No wonder the Bible says: "And they worshipped the dragon which gave power unto the beast: and they worshipped the beast, saying, Who is like unto the beast? Who is able to make war with him? And all that dwell upon the earth shall worship him, whose names are not written in the book of life." Revelation 13:4, 8.

41

Incredible!

No time has been lost track of. To see how the days of our week are the same as in the time of Christ, see Appendix 12.

Some ministers, who don't have one Bible text to show will say, "Don't worry about God's commandments, just worship God every day, or pick one day in seven." Some highly educated ministers have even said, "Don't worry about following the Bible, it's out of date. You just live a good life and everything will be all right." Many ministers - when asked why they meet on Sunday instead of the seventh day, will honestly say, "I know that Saturday is the seventh-day Sabbath of the Bible, and God hasn't changed it, but if I were to tell the people that, I'd lose my job!"

But it was fear of losing his job and getting in trouble that caused Pilate to do what he did! Remember? When the people shouted, "If thou let this man go, thou art not Caesar's friend" (John 19:12), Pilate was scared. If the people turned against him for letting Jesus go, no telling what might happen. It would cost him his job! The record says, "And so Pilate, willing to content the people, released Barabbas unto them, and delivered Jesus, when he had scourged Him, to be crucified." Mark 15:15.

That's heavy!

Again I say - no marvel that the world wonders after and worships the beast - no marvel! To save their jobs or to save their necks people compromise.

I praise God that many who are learning these truths are honest enough to come back to the Bible and follow Jesus all the way home. God makes it so plain - even a child can understand.

Only those who love our Heavenly Father and His dear Son with all their hearts, will stand through the last days and not worship the beast or receive his "mark."

By the way - the dreaded "mark of the beast" - what is it? Get ready for a shock.

42

The MARK of the BEAST 5

STOP! IF YOU HAVEN'T READ CHAPTER 2, "THE BEAST IDENTIFIED," DON'T READ THIS CHAPTER.

The "Mark of the Beast" and the "Seal of God" are direct opposites. In the end, everyone will have one or the other.

Those who choose the seal of God, will be with Jesus in His wonderful kingdom - that gorgeous paradise of beauty beyond our wildest dreams. It's a land where love, peace, and happiness reign. Those who choose the mark of the beast will be cast into the lake of fire.

Man! If there's anything we <u>don't</u> want - it's the mark of the beast!

Now we're ready to discover the hoax of all hoaxes - the counterfeit that will deceive the world and plunge it into eternal despair. It will be "the straw that broke the camel's back." Listen to what God has to say about this dreaded "mark."

"And the third angel followed them, saying with a loud voice, If any man worship the beast and his image, and receive his mark in his forehead, or in his hand, the same shall drink of the wine of the wrath of God, which is poured out without mixture into the cup of His indignation, and he shall be tormented with fire and brimstone in the presence of the holy angels and in the presence of the Lamb." Revelation 14:9, 10.

There are two easy ways to learn what the mark of the beast is -

1) Ask the beast what the mark of its authority is. It will tell you quite frankly.

2) Find what the "seal of God" is, and you'll know that the "mark of the beast" is just the opposite.

The reason why such a terrible warning is given against receiving this "mark" is - because to receive it is a great sin against God. This is why those who receive it will be lost. Those who choose the seal of God will be showing their love and loyalty to Him instead of to the beast - even in the face of death! Oh yes, the Bible reveals that pressure will be applied (the beast's favorite method). Those who refuse it will be persecuted, boycotted, not allowed to buy or sell, and finally sentenced to death!

Look now at these amazing words, and notice that this time it will be the "image of the beast" that will enforce the death decree - "And he had power to give life unto the image of the beast, that the image of the beast should both speak, and cause that as many as would not worship the image of the beast should be killed . . . And that no man might buy or sell, save he that had the mark, or the name of the beast, or the number of his name." Revelation 13:15, 17.

What a picture!

No matter which way you look at it, a crisis is stealing upon our world! People can sense it. And it won't be long.

Those who love God with all of their hearts will not conform to the pressure - come what may. They'll stand firm in the face of death, and receive the seal of the living God in their foreheads. Is this your choice? It's no trivial thing - it's a matter of eternal life, or just the opposite. Concerning God's seal it says:

"And I saw another angel ascending from the east, having the seal of the living God: and he cried with a loud voice to the four angels, to whom it was given to hurt the earth and the sea, saying, Hurt not the earth, neither the sea, nor the trees, till we have sealed the servants of our God in their foreheads." Revelation 7:2, 3.

"Winds" in prophecy stand for strife and war. A global war is coming, as we'll soon see. But here, the angels are holding it back until the servants of God can have a chance to receive His seal. It would have all broken loose before now but God in His great love and mercy, is holding it back - only a little longer.

And there have been "smoke screens." Nations have been talking "peace" while preparing for "high tech" war. "Peace, peace" is cried, when "there is no peace."

It's no accident that the "mark of the beast" hasn't yet been enforced. But soon the angels will start to let loose! Whether by T.V., radio, internet, or by seeing the persecution of others in the courts who have God's seal, people will learn the difference between the "seal" and the "mark" – and will take their stand. This very book may be one method God has chosen for you to learn these fantastic facts! It's no coincidence that you are reading it now. God is waiting for the sincere, humble followers of Jesus to learn the great issues involved - and to receive His seal, which Satan has tried to keep from them.

When all learn the issues, and make their final choice - it's closing time! Then comes the close of probation for the human race, the seven last plagues, and earth's last, stupendous battle. (We'll look at these things in a minute). Where you stand then is determined by the choice you make now! Are you ready? Here we go –

45

First of all, what is God's "seal?" A seal is something having to do with legal affairs. A law is stamped with the seal of the ruling government. A seal has three parts:

1) The name of the ruler.
2) The ruler's title.
3) The territory over which he rules.

When the government seal is on a law, or on currency, it is official. The whole loyal nation stands behind it. God's seal makes His law official, and the whole, loyal universe stands behind it.

Anyone disloyal to the seal of the government, and to the law upon which it is attached, is looked upon as being disloyal to the government itself.

Just as a government ruler's seal is placed in his law to make it official, God's seal is in His law. Here's what God says: "Bind up the testimony, seal the law among my disciples." Isaiah 8:16.

Where are we sealed? In the forehead. His law is in our hearts. Under the new covenant, His promise is:

"This is the covenant that I will make with them after those days, saith the Lord, I will put my laws into their hearts, and in their minds will I write them." Hebrews 10:16.

The Holy Spirit places the seal of God in our foreheads when we choose it. The forehead contains the "frontal lobe." This section of the brain is where our conscience is. When you receive the seal of God in your forehead, it means you have it in your conscience. You believe in it. You're loyal to it.

Just as the government ruler uses his "seal" of government to enforce the laws of the land, God uses His "seal" to enforce His law. The beast will use his seal (mark), to try to enforce his law in place of God's law.

Where will you find the seal of God with its three parts? In the very center of His law. Take a close look:

46

"Remember the Sabbath day to keep it holy. Six days shalt thou labour and do all thy work: But the seventh day is the Sabbath of the Lord thy God: in it thou shalt not do any work ... For in six days the Lord made heaven and earth, the sea, and all that in them is, and rested the seventh day: wherefore the Lord blessed the Sabbath day and hallowed it." Exodus 20:8-11.

This is the only place in the Bible where you will find God's seal. Here are the three parts of the seal:

1) His name - "the Lord."

2) His title - "thy God" (Creator).

3) His territory - "heaven and earth, the sea, and all that in them is."

This is fantastic! No wonder Satan has worked so hard to hide the truth of the sacred Sabbath from us. It's God's sign!

You may ask "Is the Sabbath really the seal of God?" Look at Ezekiel 20:12. "Moreover also I gave them my Sabbaths, to be a sign between me and them, that they might know that I am the Lord that sanctify them." "And hallow my Sabbaths; and they shall be a sign between me and you, that ye may know that I am the Lord your God." Ezekiel 20:20. (The word "sign" means the same as "seal" - see Romans 4:11).

What could be clearer? The seal of God is His Sabbath.

Satan knew that he had to get at this very part. No wonder the "beast" of Revelation ripped it out and put in a substitute! Look at this shocking statement concerning the beast's terrible act - "Of course the Catholic Church claims that the change was her act. And the act {get this now} is a mark of her ecclesiastical power and authority in religious matters."[1] Sunday worship is the mark of the Papacy's authority. The "mark." Sunday worship is the "mark of the beast!"

The issues are plain. God says that He is the true God. He has given His Sabbath as a sign of His authority as the Creator

47

of all. By keeping it, we recognize His authority. But the Catholic church says in effect:

"No! Keep the first day of the week, and lo, the entire civilized world bows in reverent obedience to the command of the holy Catholic church."[2] "It's the MARK of our authority to over-rule God's law."

But what about all of our loved ones who are keeping Sunday and don't know any better? Do they have the mark of the beast?

No! Only those who know better and realize that they are breaking God's fourth commandment are held accountable. The Bible says, "Therefore to him that knoweth to do good, and doeth it not, to him it is sin." James 4:17. You and I know now and are held accountable. Soon all will know. God is making this very point a great test for the world in the last days. It will separate those who really love God enough to obey Him, {even amid persecution} from those who merely claim to be Christians, but like Pilate, will compromise, go along with the crowd - and end up with the mark of the beast. The "Mark" won't officially be received until it is enforced by the "two horned beast" of Revelation 13.

We certainly don't want to hurt our loving Savior by breaking any of His commandments. That would break His heart. Sin hurts Him most of all. He suffered agony on the cross to take away our sins. Blood ran from His body. His love for us is very tender. Those who willfully receive the mark of the beast are willing to hurt the loving heart of God. As we choose to keep all of His commandments, it makes Him glad.

As you begin to keep His 7th day Sabbath holy, He will make it the happiest day of the week for you. You'll be able to lay aside your cares and labors one whole day and have a beautiful rest with Jesus - not only physically, but a rest of soul, a joyful peace and freedom from guilt.

If you are working in your job on God's Sabbath now, He will help you with that too. I've never seen it fail. Those who determine to keep His Sabbath holy and not work on Saturday have God's special care and miraculous providence. He will either help you get the Sabbath off from work, or if you have to lose your job, He will give you a better one! I guarantee it. That's God! That's our kind Heavenly Father.

People in every nation on earth will be tested on this very point. Millions around the world have discovered these amazing truths just like you have, and are rejoicing in a closer walk with Jesus than ever before.

Here's another question - what does it mean to receive the mark in your hand?

Remember, to receive it in the forehead means that you believe in it, you're loyal to it. (There will also be an outward sign of some kind whereby people will be able to tell who has the mark and who doesn't. We'll study that in a minute). To receive it in the hand means that when the mark is enforced by the "image of the beast," they go along with it, not because they believe in it, but just to be able to buy and sell - to keep their jobs, and save their lives. The hand is a symbol of work and making a living.

This is a shocking thought! How could anything like that happen in our free country? If the "image of the beast" tries to force everyone to receive the "mark of the beast," how does he do it?

Who is the "image of the beast" anyway?

The Image of the Beast
The Image of the Beast
The Image of the Beast
The Image of the Beast

The Image of the Beast

Who is the "image of the beast?"

What does it do?

Who gives it power? It gets more explosive as we go. It's all in Revelation 13. Here's the picture –

"And I beheld another beast coming up out of the earth; {we've already learned that this is the United States} and he had two horns like a lamb, and he spake as a dragon. And he exerciseth all the power of the first beast before him and causeth the earth and them which dwell therein to worship the first beast, whose deadly wound was healed . . . and he had power to give life unto the image of the beast that the image of the beast should both speak, and cause that as many as would not worship the image of the beast should be killed. And he causeth all, both small and great, rich and poor, free and bond, to receive a mark in their right hand, or in their foreheads: And that no man might buy or sell, save he that had the mark, or the name of the beast, or the number of his name." Revelation 13:11, 12, 15-17.

What a picture! Even though it seems impossible, God's word says it will happen.

First let me say that I love my country. I just got back from Europe, and it's great to be back. But this is what God's word says.

The United States (the two horned beast), will cause all to worship the first beast by enforcing the "mark" of the first beast by law! The word "cause" in the original Greek means "force."

A national Sunday law will be enforced in our country. In chapter one we've already seen that it's coming, and some of the reasons why.

We've already learned that, 1) the "two horned beast" is the U.S. and 2) the first beast is the Papacy. The "image of the beast" is a religious power much like the Papacy {in the U.S.}, teaching many of the same false teachings. The "image" of the beast is the majority of the Protestant world.

To say it plainly, Revelation 13 is revealing to us the astonishing fact that "Protestant America" will cause all to worship the Papacy and receive its "mark" by passing a national Sunday law, and that all who do not go along with it will suffer the consequences!

When man reaches the depth of spiritual decay and passes that law, it will not only make an "image" to the beast in our country - and copy the old papal principle of persecution, it will set up the procedure for all to receive the "mark of the beast!"[1]

It's coming clear! You see, it won't be the beast which enforces its "mark" by law in our country, it will be its "image" - Protestant America.

It all boils down to our being forced to either obey the laws of our beloved country and disobey God, or having to violate the laws of the land in order to obey our Lord. That's a real test! If you are faithful and true to God, you'll find yourself, {for a short time before Christ comes} without a job, without the right to buy or sell, and even under the death penalty!

Does this sound impossible? It's already in progress!

Large religious groups such as the Lord's Day Alliance

51

want it, and already have articles in print concerning it. Is the principle of "separation of church and state" crumbling?

The national Catholic journal, <u>Catholic Twin Circle,</u> said, "All Americans would do well to petition the President and the Congress to make a Federal law - an amendment to the Constitution if need be - to re-establish the Sabbath [meaning Sunday] as a national Day of Rest."[2]

These powerful groups have genuine concerns. They're working for many good things - better T.V. programs, to save the family, etc. But what they don't realize is that when the U.S. actually passes a national Sunday law, it has taken away the religious freedom of those who choose to keep God's day instead of the day of the sun which the Roman church brought in from pagan sun worship - it is enforcing the "mark of the beast!" Those who go along with this oppressive law while knowing what they are doing will most definitely receive the "mark of the beast." Why?

Because they will be disobeying the commandment of God in order to obey the tradition of men. Jesus said, "In vain do they worship me, teaching for doctrine the commandments of men." Mark 7:7.

Don't get me wrong. I love my country. I'm just sharing the facts.

If your head is still spinning at the shock of a future nationwide Sunday law and persecution in our country, all I can say is - draw close to God! - closer than you've ever been in your life! Fill your mind with the Bible instead of the T.V. and a thousand other things! Pray like you've never prayed before. He will help you! These things are coming with swift surety.

Believe it or not, in Virginia, my home state, it's already been done - - I mean a mandatory Sunday law - and the death sentence!

Get this shocking quote.

In 1610, the first Sunday law in America, in Virginia, required: "Every man and woman shall repair in the morning to the divine service and sermons preached upon the Sabbath [Sunday], and in the afternoon to divine service, and catechizing, upon pain for the first fault to lose their provision and the allowance for the whole week following; for the second, to lose the said allowance and also be whipped; and for the third to suffer death."!!! Laws and Orders, Divine, Politique, and Martial, for the Colony in Virginia: first established by Sir Thomas Gates, knight, Lieutenant - General, the 24th of May, 1610.

Did you know that Sunday blue laws are still on the books in Virginia and other states?

"It's unconstitutional," said a lawyer living in Richmond, VA. (speaking of the Sunday law there). "It's a religious law and it's unconstitutional." But it's still there!

Most states have had these "Sunday blue laws" enforced on and off throughout the last two hundred years. They come and go. Many lie dormant - waiting.

Do you see? God knows what He is talking about and has given us warning - a warning of love.

I.D. cards, numbers - something like this will allow the followers of the national Sunday law to buy and sell. They will have these "temporary" benefits. Tremendous pressure will be on - to conform.

Terrorism and crime will be major factors. They are shooting out of control. People are scared. People are angry at these horrors – and these things are helping to bring back the death sentence. Why, just a few hours ago I stopped at the post office. After seeing the headlines of the newspaper, I had to get one. The headlines read, "KILLER ORDERED EXECUTED."

A young man was ordered to be executed for murdering a two-year old little girl of Wildwood, Florida. The infant was kidnapped, molested, and buried alive. You can see why, with crimes of this horrible magnitude {and with terrorist

53

bombings and other horrors} the death sentence is coming back.

The judge himself pronounced that it was proved that "The capital felony was especially heinous, wicked, evil, atrocious, and cruel." Citrus Chronicle News.

"Several of the young man's family members," the paper said, "kissed and hugged the prosecutor after the proceedings were over."

The Bible in many places pronounces the death sentence for the crimes of murder, rape, witchcraft, homosexuality, etc. (Genesis 9:5,6; Deuteronomy 22:25-29; Leviticus 20:13; Exodus 22:18). Last year less than 400 people were on death row in the U.S. Now the figure tops 1100! Public opinion, only recently against capital punishment, now favors it two to one. According to Bible prophecy it will come back.

Of all horrors! It will come back and be used against those who love and obey God! "And he had power to give life unto the image of the beast, that the image of the beast should both speak, and cause as many as would not worship the image of the beast should be killed." Revelation 13:15.

Just days ago, on a city street in Atlantic City, New Jersey, a group of people talked with a man who keeps the Bible Sabbath. They said to him (Tony is his name), "What would you do if you were forced to worship on Sunday now instead of Saturday?" And then they added, "What if it costs you your life?"

"You can have my life," Tony said, "I'm following the Bible." Amazing! Did that group on the street know what they were saying?

Do people know what's going on? To use force is to use the methods of the "dragon."

The second reason the Sunday law has been urged is the economic crisis. You are so aware of the situation, that I don't even have to comment on it.

The third reason is the religious leaders - of all people -

54

will stir up the nation for this law which they will make people think is so needful. As stated in chapter one, already media messages and articles have been circulating all over the country urging the populace that - "There will be no relief from mounting economic disaster until Sunday is strictly enforced by government decrees and action."[3] Now you and I can see clearly that this is a fulfillment of prophecy, urging the nation to enforce the "mark of the beast!" But to the average person who knows almost nothing about the Bible, this plea sounds pretty good.

Another thing that will help it come is miracles. Have you noticed the tremendous surge of interest in the supernatural lately? God is certainly a God of miracles. And because of this, many believe that all miracles are from God. Not knowing their Bibles, they will be the more easily fooled by Satan's miracles. Get this -

"And I saw three unclean spirits like frogs come out of the mouth of the dragon, and out of the mouth of the beast, and out of the mouth of the false prophet. For they are the spirits of devils, working miracles, which go forth unto the kings of the earth and of the whole world." Revelation 16:13, 14.

The point here is that devils work miracles as well as God. By this deceptive means, the whole world will be deceived into worshiping the beast and receiving its mark. Through miracles, and Satan's angels appearing as dead loved ones - {telling people that God's Sabbath has been changed to Sunday} many will think that they have proof that the oppressive Sunday law is of God, and that they should go along with it to save the economy and the nation!

These lying miracles will fool millions who try to contact dead loved ones who are supposedly communicating from heaven. To people who don't know the plain word of God, this will be an overwhelming delusion! The Bible forbids anyone to try to contact the dead because when they do, they are inviting evil spirits to speak to them. This is why people who did this type of thing in Bible times were put to death. The Bible says, "The dead know not anything." Ecclesiastes 9:5. And I Thessalonians 4:16 teaches that the righteous dead will awake on the very day that Jesus appears in the sky. So don't be fooled by a demon that looks and sounds so kind and sweet - just like a dead loved one! People in our modern society will fall into this very pit! Already Satan is setting things up for it.

According to the Greeley poll, one in four Americans have tried to contact the dead! And half of the widows in America and Iceland admit to communication with the dead!"[4] {If they only knew who and what they were talking with, they might faint!}

In order to pass a national Sunday law, the constitution must first be affected. The grand principle of separation of church and state, must first be undermined (especially the first amendment).

Have you noticed anyone trying to undermine the first amendment lately? In recent years, many states requested a constitutional convention to change it. They came close to getting it! It's alarming that many leaders don't believe the separation of church and state even exists in the constitution! According to Bible prophecy, it will be repudiated. But God expects His children to do all they can to hold it back. The pilgrims shed their blood to provide for us a nation free from religious persecution and intolerance. Should we see our religious freedom go down the drain and do nothing?

The churches which have Sunday in common will unite in a grand movement so that the world can be converted. Already, religious leaders have been getting their church people into politics. (Since the national Sunday law will be a religious law, it makes sense for the devil to get the churches into politics, and try to collapse the separation of church and state - to get federal money for religious schools, and get "good" religious laws!) It's shocking, but many political as well as religious leaders are against the separation of church and state now. Have you noticed it? They're not trying to hide it! The Sunday law will be seen as just the thing to solve the horrendous problems we're facing, and to unite the whole Christian world.

Cold chills went down my spine as, in the middle of the night, on a powerful AM station near Washington, D.C., I heard a deep voice. Cold as steel, it proclaimed that the curse of God rests upon us and will not be removed until the nation repents, and turns back to God by keeping Sunday holy! It will be the religious leaders to a large degree who will compel all to "worship the first beast." To worship the first beast, you don't have to join the Catholic church. All you would have to do is follow the mark of its authority instead of the sign of God's authority - and you would be honoring that power more than God; in His sight - worshiping it. Atrocities of the dark ages will be repeated! Society is being manipulated to the degree that in the near future, to receive the "mark of the beast" will be the popular thing to do! - "And all the world wondered after the beast. And they worshiped the dragon which gave power unto the beast: and they worshiped the beast, saying, Who is like unto the beast? Who is able to make war with him?" Revelation 13:3,4.

Those who dare oppose this law will be seen as "rejects of society." One of the worst things you can say about a person is to call him a member of a "cult" or a "sect." Those who oppose the mark of the beast will be seen as "cultists" of the worst kind. They'll be worked with by the authorities. When fines and all manner of economic boycotts have failed, then they will be sentenced to death. Revelation 13:15-17.

Men, women, and children from all walks of life will be fleeing for their lives and hiding in the most desolate areas; or, if caught, cast into jails to await the penalty. War, strife, and terrible calamities of nature will be blamed on them. Like their Savior, and millions of martyrs before them, they'll be rejected by loved ones, mocked, and looked upon as the "poor fools who have brought all this trouble on us."

As those loyal to God are brought to court for their faith, the issues about God's true Sabbath will spread around the world! The truth of God's fourth commandment will be seen in contrast with the counterfeit day which the image of the beast is trying to enforce by law. Notwithstanding the terrorism, pleasure seeking, and chaos of the world, all will be led to receive either the "seal of God" or the "mark of the beast."

Spirits of devils go out to deceive the whole world {Rev. 16:13,14}. Those who make the word of God their guide will not fall for this world-wide hoax. They will discover the truth about Jesus' holy day, and will observe it in obedience and loving gratitude - even in the face of mockery and death.

Then - when all have decided {which won't be long}, the close of probation comes and Jesus pronounces the most solemn sentence - "He that is unjust, let him be unjust still; and he which is filthy, let him be filthy still: and he that is righteous, let him be righteous still: and he that is holy, let him be holy still." Revelation 22:11.

Every case has been decided for life or death. Then - the seven last, terrible plagues of Revelation 16 are poured out upon the wicked, and a global conflict takes place under the sixth plague. No matter which way you look at this thing, a great crisis is stealing upon our world. This global conflict will be like nothing you've ever dreamed of before - your wildest imagination has never pictured it.

What will it be like?

THE GLOBAL CONFLICT
THE GLOBAL CONFLICT

*S*hakespeare wrote: "There is a line by us unseen that crosses every path, the hidden boundary between God's patience and His wrath."

"A great crisis awaits the people of God. A crisis awaits the world. The most momentous struggle of all the ages is just before us."[1] "At that time shall Michael stand up, the great Prince which standeth for the children of thy people: and there shall be a time of trouble, such as never was since there was a nation even to that same time: and at that time thy people shall be delivered, everyone that shall be found written in the book." Daniel 12:1.

When the great warning of Revelation 14:9,10 against receiving the mark of the beast has finished its work, and all have made up their minds, probation closes. God's people have received the great outpouring of the Holy Spirit - "the refreshing from the presence of the Lord." And they're prepared for the trying ordeal ahead. They are sealed with the "seal of the Living God." The wicked are finally left to the master they've chosen. They've rejected God's mercy, despised His tender love, and trampled on His law. Now - unprotected from Satan's insane wrath, they have no shelter from his power. He will then plunge the entire world into one great, final trouble spoken of in Daniel 12. God's wrath poured out on this planet in rebellion will come in the form of the seven last plagues brought to view in Revelation 16. Just as the ten plagues of Egypt were against the gods that they worshiped, so, the seven last plagues will be especially focused against those who worship the beast and his image.

As we study this stupendous subject and try to see the whole picture, we find that God is so fair, so kind - and those upon whom these plagues fall are so disobedient, so hateful, that no one in the entire on-looking universe will accuse God of being unfair for judging thus. After the first three devastating plagues an angel says, "Thou art righteous Oh Lord, . . . because thou hast judged thus. For they have shed the blood of saints and prophets, and Thou hast given them blood to drink; for they are worthy." Revelation 16:5,6.

The heaven-defying law has been passed and God's obedient people have been persecuted, mocked, and sentenced to death. And now -

"I heard a great voice out of the temple saying to the seven angels, Go your ways, and pour out the vials of the wrath of God upon the earth. And the first angel went, and poured out his vial upon the earth; and there fell a noisome and grievous sore upon the men which had the mark of the beast, and upon them which worshipped his image." Revelation 16:1, 2.

Can you imagine sores all over your body!

Notice, these gnawing, painful sores will afflict only those who have the mark of the beast and worship his image. What will it be like when this happens?

Can you picture the news telling the shocking story of this gross epidemic? People by the millions who have received the "mark" for the purpose of saving their jobs and comforts of life now find that their comfort is gone!

Instead of causing them to repent, and pray to God for forgiveness, these terrible sores only cause them to "blaspheme God" and "gnaw their tongues for pain."

God knows that if He gave them a million years more, they

wouldn't change. When the plagues begin to fall, you'll know that every case is decided for eternity, and that probation is closed - forever. Medical science will be helpless then. Can you picture doctors' offices and drug stores packed with shouting, angry, crying victims? What medicine will relieve the throbbing, biting pain?

Not everyone will get these awful sores. Those who so lately have been persecuted and mocked, are now safe. Angels of God protect them. They have loved and been obedient to their Lord even unto death, and now Jesus is very close to them. Though they'll be sentenced to death, God's people will not die. Jesus will interpose to save them. While the wicked are perishing with pestilence and famine, God's people are sheltered in the shadow of His hand.

All of a sudden the news breaks - the waters have turned to blood!

"And the second angel poured out his vial upon the sea; and it became as the blood of a dead man: and every living soul died in the sea." Revelation 16:3. Under the third plague the rivers also turn to blood. The word "soul" here means "living creature."

Have you ever seen the blood of a dead man? It coagulates into a jelly mass. Those who have hated God's people have tried to shed their blood. Now, picture them in the pain of their feverish boils turning on their faucets for some relief, and out comes the oozing "blood of a dead man."

"And I heard another out of the altar say, even so, Lord God Almighty, true and righteous are Thy judgments." Revelation 16:7.

Look at the beaches! Men are afraid. Where will they drink? They've tried to shed the blood of the obedient. Now they have blood to drink.

Now something unbelievable happens. The atmospheric layer that shields the earth from the scorching heat fails.

"And the fourth angel poured out his vial upon the sun; and power was given unto him to scorch men with fire. And

61

men were scorched with great heat, and blasphemed the name of God, which hath power over these plagues: and they repented not to give Him glory." Revelation 16:8, 9.

Horrible pain is now experienced by the wicked. The combination of scorching heat and raw sores is excruciating.

Miracles will abound, like in Moses' day; some from God, some from Satan. The wicked will not realize that the devil has counterfeited the gifts of the Spirit. Many who have worked miracles and done wonderful works, have trampled on God's Sabbath and persecuted those who honored it. They've felt secure in God's favor. But now their rage is great.

Concerning the disobedient, Jesus said, "Not every one that saith unto me, Lord, Lord, shall enter into the kingdom of heaven; but he that doeth the will of My Father which is in heaven. Many will say to me in that day, Lord, Lord, have we not prophesied in Thy name? and in Thy name done many wonderful works? And then will I profess unto them, I never knew you: depart from me, ye that work iniquity." Matthew 7:21-23. Now their true character is revealed. They "blaspheme God and repent not."

Air conditioners will not be able to cope with the intense heat. The buildings will be like ovens. For the wicked, there'll be no relief anywhere.

This plague is perfectly suited to the sin of the people. They've honored the "day of the sun" according to the traditions of men - and now God gives them sun! The New English Bible says that men were "fearfully burned" during the fourth plague.

In that day, many will long for the shelter of God's mercy which they have so long despised.

God's people will still be hiding in desolate places, but He who provided food for Elijah in the wilderness will care for them. While the wicked are dying from the pestilence, angels will shield God's faithful people and supply their wants. God's promise is - "When the poor and needy seek water, and there is none, and their tongue faileth for thirst, I the Lord will hear them, I the God of Israel will not forsake them." Isaiah 41:17.

While the disobedient are shrieking in pain, reeking with sweat, and their parched throats are raw for thirst, God's promise to His people is: "The Lord is thy keeper: the Lord is thy shade upon thy right hand. The sun shall not smite thee by day, nor the moon by night." Psalms 121:5, 6.

In choosing to honor the beast and receive his "mark" instead of honoring God and His "seal," the people have chosen darkness. Now again, God gives them what they've chosen.

"And the fifth angel poured out his vial upon the seat of the beast; and his kingdom was full of darkness; and they gnawed their tongues for pain, and blasphemed the God of heaven because of their pains and their sores, and repented not of their deeds." Revelation 16:10, 11.

Can you imagine that! I think the human mind is inadequate to conceive of the horror that will engulf all society. People of high society; the rich; men of science; and the ignorant masses will be paralyzed with pain, hate, and panic. Society will be utter chaos! Of these scourges the Bible says: "The land mourneth; . . . because the harvest of the field is perished . . . All the trees of the field are withered: because joy is withered away from the sons of men." "How do the beasts groan! The herds of cattle are perplexed, because they have no pasture." Joel 1:10-12, 18. Oh, if they had only responded to God's great kindness. His arms have been stretched out in love. Now it's too late.

The disobedient have decreed that those who've received God's seal cannot buy or sell. Now they themselves are starving with famine and groping in utter darkness. This supernatural darkness is a fit symbol of the gross darkness that has come upon the minds of those who have turned away from the light of truth.

God's people are still hiding out. They've weeks ago lost their jobs, homes, and fled for their lives before insane men urged on by the religious leaders and evil angels. They've given up all for Christ. They've seen the wicked perishing while angels of God provided food for them. To the obedient God's promise is given - "Bread shall be given him; his waters shall be sure." "A thousand shall fall at thy side, and ten thousand at thy right hand; but it shall not come nigh thee. Only with thine eyes shalt thou behold and see the reward of the wicked . . . there shall no evil befall thee, neither shall any plague come nigh thy dwelling." Isaiah 33:16; Psalms 91:3-10.

By the fifth plague, the whole wicked world is really angry. They've decided that those who honor God's Sabbath of the Bible are the cause of the horrible convulsions of nature, and they determine to blot them from the earth!

The date is set. When the clock strikes midnight on a certain day, God's obedient people will be sentenced to death!

To all appearances it seems that the doom of the people of God is fixed. Day and night they cry to God for deliverance. Has God forsaken them? This very experience prepares them for the bliss of heaven as nothing else could.

In the midst of the chaos, the sixth angel pours out his vial - "And the sixth angel poured out his vial upon the great river Euphrates; and the water thereof was dried up, that the way of the kings of the east might be prepared. And I saw three unclean spirits like frogs come out of the mouth of the dragon, and out of the mouth of the beast, and out of the mouth of the false prophet. For they are spirits of devils working miracles, which go forth unto the kings of the earth and of the whole world, to gather them to the battle of that great day of God Almighty." "And he gathered them together into a place called in the Hebrew tongue Armageddon." Revelation 16:12-14, 16.

Here's where the spirits of devils, by their miracles, prepare the rulers and people of the world, and "gather them together" to fight against God and His people. This is the global conflict. This is the battle of Armageddon. It's earth's final battle between good and evil. All have taken sides. The wicked are in the majority and seemingly have great advantage - like David against Goliath.

The word "Armageddon" is made of two Hebrew words - "Har" and "Megiddon." This is not just a local battle fought in the Valley of Megiddo. The word "Har" means "mountain." "Armageddon" is the word to denote the great universal battle where the wicked turn against God and His faithful people. This is a world-wide battle. The national Sunday law of the U.S. has spread to all the nations of the world. The universal law seeks in one day - to strike a decisive blow that will wipe the hated sect from the face of the earth.

When the great, corrupt Christian coalition of the world comes to the place where it causes (amid miracles and Satanic delusion) the leaders ("kings of the earth") to decree that those who will not go along with the Sunday law should be put to death, it brings the world to the place of sealing its own doom.

The people of God, some still in prison, some hidden in forests and mountains - still plead for God's protection, while companies of armed men, hurried on by evil angels, are preparing to execute the death sentence. It's now - in the darkest hour, that the God of Israel will interpose to deliver His faithful people.

The date has been set to strike one stunning blow that will wipe the hated sect from the face of the earth. At midnight the death decree goes into effect. At midnight - the Mighty God of heaven will interpose to save His people.[2]

Watch what happens -

"And the seventh angel poured out his vial into the air; and there came a great voice out of the temple of heaven, from the throne, saying, It is done. And there were voices, and thunders and lightnings; and there was a great earthquake, such as was not since men were upon the earth, so mighty an earthquake and so great. And the great city was divided into three parts, and the cities of the nations fell: and great Babylon came in remembrance before God, to give unto her the cup of the wine of the fierceness of his wrath. And every island fled away, and the mountains were not found. And there fell upon men a great hail out of heaven, every stone about the weight of a talent: and men blasphemed God because of the plague of the hail; for the plague was exceeding great." Revelation 16:17-21.

BABYLON THE GREAT - THE MOTHER OF HARLOTS has caused all nations to drink of the wine of her mixture of Christian and sun-worshiping practices. Now she drinks of the wine of the wrath of God.

Satan's attempt to enforce the death decree against God's humble people is the final climax in his king of swindles. God steps in to save His people. And what a deliverance!

Everything in nature goes haywire. The mountains shake like reeds in the wind. The wicked are paralyzed with abject terror and look with amazement upon the scene, while the obedient watch with solemn joy at the signs of their deliverance. Ragged rocks are hurled in every direction. The sea is lashed into fury. The earth heaves and swells. Its surface is breaking apart. Mountain chains sink. Islands disappear. Wicked cities that have become like Sodom are swallowed up by tidal waves. Great hailstones, each "about the weight of a talent" are wreaking havoc. A talent is about 63 pounds. You can see that these, like cannon balls, will beat the wicked cities to a pulp.

Splendid mansions erected by the rich with money embezzled from the poor are dashed to pieces before their eyes. Prison walls tumble down, and God's humble people, who have been held in bondage for their faith are set free.

It's impossible to describe the horror and despair of those who have trampled on God's requirements. The enemies of God's law, from the ministers down, have a new conception of what is truth. Too late, they see the true nature of the counterfeit sabbath that the Roman church has brought in, and the shaky foundation they've been building on. Many now see that they're lost. They've chosen the easy, popular way - and have received the mark of the beast. They've followed the religious leaders instead of the plain word of God. They've been led to believe that the majority couldn't be wrong. Now they turn on their ministers and bitterly reproach them for their sorry state.[3]

The global conflict has prepared the way for the coming of Christ and His mighty host of angels during the last of the plagues. And what a scene! - -

There appears in the sky a cloud which betokens the coming of the "King of Kings and Lord of Lords." In solemn silence God's people gaze upon it as it draws nearer and nearer to the earth. Brighter and brighter it becomes, and more glorious, until it's a great white cloud, its glory like consuming fire. Jesus rides forth as a mighty conqueror. "And the armies which were in heaven" follow Him. Revelation 19:11,14. The whole heaven seems filled with dazzling forms - "ten thousand times ten thousand, and thousands of thousands." No pen can describe it. No human mind is adequate to imagine the fantastic and holy scene. As the living cloud comes still nearer, every eye beholds the lovely Jesus. There's no crown of thorns on that holy brow, but now a crown of glory rests upon His sacred head. His face outshines the dazzling brightness of the sun.

"And He hath on His vesture and on His thigh a name written, KING OF KINGS, AND LORD OF LORDS." Revelation 19:16. As the King of Glory descends on the cloud amid terrific majesty, and wrapped in flaming fire, the earth trembles. The ground heaves and swells, and the very mountains move from their foundations. "Our God shall come, and shall not keep silence: a fire shall devour before Him, and it shall be very tempestuous round about Him. He shall call to the heavens from above, and to the earth, that He may judge His people." Psalms 50:3, 4.

"And the kings of the earth, and the great men, and the rich men, and the chief captains, and the mighty men, and every bondman, and every free man hid themselves in the dens and in the rocks of the mountains; and said to the mountains and rocks, Fall on us, and hide us from the face of Him that sitteth on the throne, and from the wrath of the Lamb: for the great day of His wrath is come; and who shall be able to stand?" Revelation 6:15-17.

The jokes have stopped. Cursing, lying lips are now silent. In the midst of their terror the wicked hear the voices of God's people joyfully exclaiming: "Lo this is our God; we have waited for Him, and He will save us." Isaiah 25:9.

While the earth is reeling like a drunkard; amid the terrific roar of thunder, and upheavals of nature, the voice of the Son of God calls His faithful ones of all ages from the grave.

"For the Lord himself shall descend from heaven with a shout, with the voice of the archangel, and with the trump of God: and the dead in Christ shall rise first: Then we which are alive and remain shall be caught up together with them in the clouds to meet the Lord in the air: and so shall we ever be with the Lord." 1 Thessalonians 4:16, 17.

God's living people are changed "in a moment, in the twinkling of an eye." I Corinthians 15:51, 52. The righteous who have been raised from the dead, and the living who have just been changed, are "caught up to meet the Lord in the air." I Thessalonians 4:17. Angels "gather together His elect from the four winds, from one end of heaven to the other." Little children are carried by holy angels to their mother's arms. Friends long separated by death are united, nevermore to part - and with songs of gladness ascend together to the city of God.[4] Praise God friend! What a Saviour!

I sincerely believe that there's no way for you to read these amazing truths of God's word without having a deep longing to follow Christ all the way and have a part in His glorious kingdom. I know that you would have never read this unusual book this far unless you had a real interest in learning truth and following Jesus all the way.

You've learned some of Satan's tactics, and how he will trick the world into accepting his greatest hoax. You've learned how to escape receiving the mark of the beast, and something of God's great love and mercy in giving us the warning. Now you see that the corrupt woman of Revelation 17, named "Babylon," is the great body of fallen Christianity which has become a mixture of truth and sun-worshiping practices from ancient Babylon. You can see that in Revelation 18:4, when God says, "Come out of her My people, that ye be not partakers of her sins, and that ye receive not of her plagues," He's calling you. It's a love call. It's God's last call to all born-again believers to separate themselves from organizations, no matter how friendly and kind the members may be, which are not obeying Jesus fully, and keeping all of God's commandments.

Very soon, all will have made their choice for the "seal of God" or the "mark of the beast." It's not just a matter of two days, it's a matter of worship, of loyalty - either to God, or to the beast power. Now - while Jesus is pleading His blood for us in the Most Holy Place in heaven - now, when "the hour of His judgment is come" Rev. 14:7 - before our probation is closed forever, before every case is decided for life or death - even now - He is inviting us to surrender all to Him, and have life and peace. He is inviting you. Soon it will be too late.

Because the lovely Jesus shed His precious blood for me on the cross of Calvary, I choose, by the grace of God, to follow Him all the way, keep all of His commandments, including His seventh-day Sabbath, and receive the "seal of the living God." How about you? Will you choose to be true to Him too? You'll be so happy that you did! He says, "Blessed are they that do his commandments, that they may have right to the tree of life, and may enter in through the gates into the city." Revelation 22:14.

There are other major questions that come to our minds - What about the millennial reign of Christ? After the devil and the wicked are turned to ashes, will the fire of hell go out? [See Ezekiel 28:14-19, Malachi 4:3, Isaiah 47:14] What is the unpardonable sin? Why are there so many denominations?

There's not room in this small book to answer these, and many other questions that you may have. For this reason, I'm making available to you a second book entitled *Great Controversy*. This intriguing volume will answer these, and other vital questions which are helping millions prepare for Christ's soon coming. In *Great Controversy,* you'll be able to learn "Why Were Sin and Suffering Permitted?" and "Who Are the Angels?" More of Satan's plots will be exposed. You'll be able to discover if there is an organization that actually follows the requirements necessary for a group to constitute the "remnant church" of Revelation 12:17. Also, you'll thrill to discover more about what heaven will be like, and about the great outpouring of the Holy Spirit. If you would like to have your own personal copy of this most intriguing book, fill out the little order form on the next page. We will rush it to you immediately.

If the Spirit of God impresses you to help get these *National Sunday Law* books out to many precious people who need so much to know these vital things, you may order them as well. And you may write to me personally. I want to see you soon in that "land of delight," in that wonderful land called heaven, where the lovely Jesus is - "where dreams come true."

Now may our kind Father richly bless you and your dear ones as you continue to study His marvelous word! "The grace of our Lord Jesus Christ be with you all. Amen."

The author may be contacted at this same address.

Amazing Truth Publications
PO Box 68
Thompsonville IL 62890

Por favor envíeme *La Gran Controversia*
Estoy incluyendo $5.00

Nombre _____

Dirección _____

Ciudad _____ Estado_____ Código _____

Ley Dominical Nacional
formulario de pedido

Para ordenar el libro *Ley Dominical Nacional* favor de
marcar abajo la cantidad deseada. El envío es gratis.

	Cantidad	Precio Total
1-3 libros por $5.00 c/u	_____	_____
4-14 libros por $3.00 c/u	_____	_____
15-99 libros por $1.00 c/u	_____	_____
100 libros por .70¢ c/u	_____	_____
1,000 libros por .50¢ c/u	_____	_____
	Gran Total =	_____

Envía tu cheque a: Amazing Truth Publications,
PO Box 68, Thompsonville IL 62890.

Nombre _____

Dirección _____

Ciudad _____ Estado_____ Código _____

El autor puede ser contactado a la misma dirección.

APPENDIX 1

By the year 476 A.D. the Roman Empire had been broken up into exactly ten kingdoms.

"The historian Machiavelli, without the slightest reference to this prophecy, gives the following list of the nations which occupied the territory of the Western Empire at the time of the fall of Romulus Augustus (476 A.D.), the last emperor of Rome: the Lombards, the Franks, the Burgundians, the Ostrogoths, the Visigoths, the Vandals, the Heruli, the Suevi, the Huns, and the Saxons: ten in all.

"They have never since the breaking up of old Rome been united into one single empire; they have never formed one whole even like the United States. No scheme of proud ambition seeking to reunite the broken fragments has ever succeeded; when such have arisen, they have been invariably dashed to pieces.

"And the division is as apparent now as ever. Plainly and palpably inscribed on the map of Europe to this day, it confronts the skeptic with its silent but conclusive testimony to the fulfilment of this great prophecy."

The Divine Program of the World's History, by H. Grattan Guenness, pgs. 318-321. (As quoted in *Bible Readings For the Home,* Review and Herald Pub. Assoc., London, MCMXLII, pgs. 216, 217).

APPENDIX 1A

THE "BEAST" and the "LITTLE HORN"

1) The "little horn" has the "eyes of man." Daniel 7:8.

   The "beast" has the number of a man." Revelation 13:18.

2) The "little horn" "wears out the saints of the Most High." Daniel 7:25.

   The "beast" also "makes war with the saints." Revelation 13:7.

3) The "little horn" speaks "great words against the Most High." Daniel 7:25.

   The "beast" also "Opened his mouth in blasphemy against God." Revelation 13:6.

4) The "little horn" comes up among the ten horns (10 divisions of Rome). Daniel 7:8.

   The "beast" receives its "power, seat, and great authority" from Rome (after the ten divisions were formed). Revelation 13:2.

Appendix 2

The 1260 Year Reign of the Beast

The seven verses mentioning the 1260 year time period are all speaking of the same power which persecutes God's people. These texts are as follows: *Revelation 13:5, Revelation 11.2, Daniel 7.25, Revelation 12:14, Revelation 11:3, Revelation 12:6 and Daniel 12. 7.*

The key that unlocks the time prophecies is the principle given in Ezekiel 4:6 and Numbers 14:34. These verses reveal to us that one day in prophecy equals one literal year. For this reason all time prophecies must be first broken down into days. Using this Bible "key," time prophecies work out perfcctly and become easy to understand.

A month in Bible reckoning contains 30 days. A year contains 360 days. This is the formula for understanding all prophetic time.

In Revelation 11:2 and 12:14, the time given is "time," "times," and 'half a time." This equals 3½ times. From Daniel 4 we learn that a "time" equals one literal year. In that chapter you'll find that King Nebuchadnezzar lost his mind as Daniel predicted, and crawled around in the field for "seven times." He was in that condition for 7 literal years. So 3½ times equals 3½ years (3½ years contain 1260 days).

Revelation 11:3 and 12:6 plainly give the time as 1260 days (that the beast would persecute God's people).

Appendix 2 continued

Using the day for a year principle found in Ezekiel 4:6 and Numbers 14:34, we see that this power would rule for 1260 years before receiving its "deadly wound." When we take a look at the beast power, we see that this is exactly what happened. For God to repeat this time period seven times like this, shows the importance which He places on it.

Here are the verses in sequence:

Revelation 11:2 and 13:5 describe this power as reigning for 42 months. (42 months with 30 days to a month contain 1260 days.)

Daniel 7:25 and 12:7; and Revelation 12:14 describe the beast as reigning for 3½ "times," or years. (3½ prophetic years also contain 1260 days.)

Revelation 11:3 and 12:6 describe this persecuting power as reigning for 1260 days.

All seven texts describe this power as reigning for 1260 prophetic days, which is 1260 literal years.

Appendix 3

The following extracts are from authoritative works by Catholic dignitaries concerning the title and position of their leader.

"All the names which are attributed to Christ in Scripture, implying His supremacy over the church, are also attributed to the Pope." Bellamin, "On the Authority of Councils," book 2, Chapter 17.

"For thou art the shepherd, thou art the physician, thou art the director, thou art the husbandman, finally thou art another God on earth." Labbe and Cossart's "History of the Councils," Vol. XIV. col. 109.

"For the title "Lord God the Pope," see a gloss on the Extravagantes of Pope John XXII, title 14, chapter 4, Declaramus.

In an Antwerp edition of the Extravagantes, the words. "Dominum Deum Nostrum Papam" ("Our Lord God the Pope") occur in column 153. In a Paris edition, they occur in column 140.

"Hence the Pope is crowned with a triple crown, as king of heaven, and earth, and purgatory." Prompta Bibliotheca, Feraris, Vol. VI, pg. 26. article "Papa."

In a passage which is included in the Roman Catholic Canon Law, Pope Innocent III declares that the Roman pontiff is "the vicegerent upon earth, not of a mere man, but of very God;" and in a gloss on the passage it is explained that this is because he is the vicegerent of Christ, who is "very God and very man." See Decretales Domini Gregorii Papae IX (Decretals of the Lord Pope Gregory IX), liberi. de translatione Episcoporum, (on the transference of Bishops), title 7, chapter 3; Corpus Juris Canonice (2nd Leipzig ed.,1881), col. 99; (Paris, 1612), tom. 2, Decretales. col. 205.

Appendix 3 continued

INFALLIBILITY

Among the twenty-seven propositions known as the "Dictates of Hildebrand" (under the name of Pope Gregory VII) occur the following:

"2. That the Roman pontiff alone is justly styled universal.

"6. That no person... may live under the same roof with one excommunicated by the Pope.

"9. That all princes should kiss his feet only.

"19. That he can be judged by no one.

"22. That the Roman Church never erred, nor will it, according to the scripture, ever err.

"27. That he can absolve subjects from their allegiance to unrighteous rulers."

In Clark's Commentary on Daniel 7:25, it says: "They have assumed infallibility, which belongs only to God. They profess to forgive sin, which belongs only to God."

Appendix 4

THE BIBLE FORBIDDEN

In the Council of Toulouse, the church leaders ruled: "We prohibit laymen possessing copies of the Old and New Testament . . . We forbid them most severely to have the above books in the popular vernacular." "The lords of the districts shall carefully seek out the heretics in dwellings, hovels, and forests, and even their underground retreats shall be entirely wiped out." Concil Tolosanum, Pope Gregory IX, Anno. Chr. 1229.

The church Council of Tarragona ruled that: "No one may possess the books of the Old and New Testaments in the Romance language, and if anyone possesses them he must turn them over to the local bishop within eight days after the promulgation of this decree, so that they may be burned." D. Lortsch, Histoire de la Bible en France, 1910, p. 14.

After the Bible societies were formed, they were classed with Communism in an amazing decree. On December 8, 1866, Pope Pius IX, in his encyclical Quanta Cura, issued the following statement: "Socialism, Communism, clandestine societies, Bible societies . . . pests of this sort must be destroyed by all means."

Appendix 5

"WAR WITH THE SAINTS"

"Under these bloody maxims, those persecutions were carried on, from the eleventh and twelfth centuries almost to the present day, (written in 1845), which stand out on the page of history. After the signal of open martyrdom had been given in the canons of Orleans, these followed the extirpation of the Albigenses under the form of a crusade, the establishment of the Inquisition, the cruel attempts to extinguish the Waldenses, the martyrdoms of the Lollards, the cruel wars to exterminate the Bohemians, the burning of Huss and Jerome, and multitudes of other confessors..., the extinction by fire and sword of the Reformation in Spain and Italy, by fraud and open persecution in Poland, and the massacre of Bartholomew, . . . besides the slow and secret murders of the holy tribunal of the Inquisition." T.R. Birks, M.A. The First Two Visions of Daniel, (London: 1845) pg. 258, 259.

"The number of the victims of the Inquisition in Spain, is given in 'The History of the Inquisition in Spain,' by Llorente, (former secretary of the Inquisition), pgs. 206-208. This authority acknowledged that more than 300,000 suffered persecution in Spain alone, of whom 31,912 died in the flames. Millions more were slain for their faith throughout Europe." Printed in *Bible Readings For the Home*, (Washington: Review & Herald Pub. Assoc., 1942) p. 221.

"The church has persecuted. Only a tyro in church history will deny that...one hundred and fifty years after Constantine, the Donatists were persecuted and sometimes put to death. . . . Protestants were persecuted in France and Spain with the full approval of the church authorities . . . When she thinks it good to use physical force, she will use it." The Western Watchmen (Roman Catholic), of St. Louis.

Appendix 6

EDICT AGAINST THE WALDENSES

"A considerable portion of the text of the papal bull issued by Innocent VIII in 1487 against the Waldenses (the original of which is in the library of the University of Cambridge) is given, in an English translation, in John Dowling's History of Romanism (1871 ed.), book 6, chapter 5; sec. 62." Taken from *Cosmic Conflict* (Washington: Review & Herald Pub. Assoc. 1982) p. 602.

Appendix 7

IMAGES

The second Council of Nicea, A.D. 787, was called to establish image worship in the church. This council is recorded in Ecclesiastical Annals, by Baronius, Vol. 9, pp. 391-407. (Antwerp, 1612); and Charles J. Hefele, *A History of the Councils of the Church From the Original Documents*, book 18, chapter 1, secs. 332, 333; chapter 2, secs. 345-352 (T. and T. Clark ed., 1896), Vol. 5, pp. 260-304, and 342-372.

J. Mendham, in *The Seventh General Council*, the Second of Nicea, Introduction, pp. iii-vi, says - "The worship of images was one of those corruptions of Christianity which crept into the church stealthily and almost without notice or observation. This corruption did not, like other heresies, develop itself at once, for in that case it would have met with decided censure and rebuke.

"Images were first introduced into churches, not to be worshiped, but either in place of books to give instruction to those who could not read, or to excite devotion in the minds of others... but it was found that images brought into churches, darkened rather than enlightened the minds of the ignorant - degraded rather than exalted the devotion of the worshiper."

APPENDIX 8

CHANGE OF GOD'S LAW

"Although the ten commandments are found in the Roman Catholic Versions of the Scriptures, yet the faithful are instructed from the catechisms of the church, and not from the Bible. As it appears (in these catechisms), the law of God has been changed and virtually re-enacted by the Papacy.

"The second commandment, which forbids the making of, and bowing down to images, is omitted in Catholic catechisms, and the tenth, which forbids coveting, is divided into two." *Bible Readings For the Home,* (Washington: Review & Herald Pub. Assoc., 1942), p. 221.

On the opposite page is God's law as given by Himself, and as changed by man.

APPENDIX 8, continued

AS GIVEN BY JEHOVAH	AS CHANGED BY MAN
I	**I**
I am the LORD thy God. Thou shalt have no other gods before Me.	I am the Lord thy God: thou shalt not have strange gods before Me.
II	**II**
Thou shalt not make unto thee any graven image, or any likeness of anything that is in heaven above, or that is in the earth beneath, or that is in the water under the earth; thou shalt not bow down thyself to them, nor serve them; for I the Lord thy God am a jealous God, visiting the iniquity of the fathers upon the children unto the third and fourth generation of them that hate Me; and showing mercy unto thousands of them that love Me, and keep My commandments.	Thou shalt not take the name of the Lord thy God in vain.
III	**III**
Thou shalt not take the name of the Lord thy God in vain: for the Lord will not hold him guiltless that taketh His name in vain.	Remember that thou keep holy the Sabbath day.
IV	**IV**
Remember the Sabbath day to keep it holy. Six days shalt thou labor and do all thy work: but the seventh day is the Sabbath of the Lord thy God: in it thou shalt not do any work, thou, nor thy son, nor thy daughter,thy manservant, nor thy maidservant, nor thy cattle, nor thy stranger that is within thy gates: for in six days the Lord made heaven and earth, the sea, and all that in them is; and rested the seventh day: wherefore the Lord blessed the Sabbath day,and hallowed it	Honor thy father and thy mother.
V	**V**
Honor thy father and thy mother: that thy days may be long upon the land which the Lord thy God giveth thee.	Thou shalt not kill.
VI	**VI**
Thou shalt not kill.	Thou shalt not commit adultery.
VII	**VII**
Thou shalt not commit adultery.	Thou shalt not steal.
VIII	**VIII**
Thou shalt not steal.	Thou shalt not bear false witness against thy neighbor.
IX	**IX**
Thou shalt not bear false witness against thy neighbor.	Thou shalt not covet thy neighbor's wife.
X	**X**
Thou shalt not covet thy neighbor's house, thou shalt not covet thy neighbor's wife,nor his manservant, nor his maidservant,nor his ox, nor his ass, nor anything that is thy neighbor's.	Thou shalt not covet thy neighbor's goods.
(Exodus 20:3-17)	**(Butler's Catechism, page 28)**

Appendix 9

THE FIRST SUNDAY LAW

"The earliest recognition of the observation of Sunday as a legal duty is a constitution of Constantine in 321 A.D. enacting that all courts of justice, inhabitants of towns, and workshops were to be at rest on Sunday (venerabili die Solis), with an exception in favor of those engaged in agricultural labor." *Encyclopedia Britannica,* ninth edition, article, "Sunday."

The Latin original is in the Codes Justiniani (Codes of Justinian), lib. 3, title 12, lex. 3.

The law is given in Latin and in English in Philip Schaff's *History of the Christian Church,* Vol. 3, 3d period, chapter 7, sec. 75, pg. 380, footnote 1.

And in Albert Henry Newman's, <u>A Manual of Church History</u>, (Philadelphia: The American Baptist Publication Society, 1933), rev. ed., Vol. 1, pp. 305-307.

And in Leroy E. Froom, *The Prophetic Faith of Our Fathers* (Washington, D.C.: Review & Herald Publishing Assoc., 1950), Vol. l, pp. 376-381.

Appendix 10

"FIRST DAY" BIBLE TEXTS

Millions of conscientious Christians attend church every Sunday, the first day of the week. They do so believing that somewhere, somehow, someone changed the day of worship.

Either that, or they aren't aware that God set aside the seventh day, not the first day of the week as His holy day.

It is true, a change has been made.

But by whom? We've discovered that God made the Sabbath during the first week of earth's history. He set it aside as a weekly appointment between man and Himself - as a blessing, a refreshment, a date between two lovers so to speak (God and man.)

If God changed His mind about His special appointment day with us, wouldn't He have recorded so momentous an adjustment in the Bible?

We've already seen that the beast power claims to have made the change, but what does the Bible say about it?

There are eight texts in the New Testament that mention the first day of the week. Look at them carefully.

> Matthew 28:1
> Mark 16:1,2
> Mark 16:9
> Luke 24:1
> John 20:1
> John 20:19
> Acts 20:7,8
> I Corinthians 16:1,2

The first five texts simply state that the women came to the sepulchre early on the resurrection morning, and that Jesus rose from the dead.

Now look up John 20:19 in your Bible. It tells us that Jesus appeared to the disciples later on the resurrection day.

It says that the reason they were assembled was "for fear of the Jews."

85

They were scared. No telling when the Jews might grab them and treat them to the same fate as their Master. They were hiding.

They had seen their beloved Master die on Friday. They "returned, and prepared spices and ointments; and rested the Sabbath day according to the commandment." Luke 23:56. And now they're hiding with the doors shut "for fear of the Jews." John 20:19. There's no mention of a change of God's holy law.

The seventh text is Acts 20:7,8. It says "and upon the first day of the week, when the disciples came together to break bread, Paul preached unto them, ready to depart on the morrow; and continued his speech until midnight. And there were many lights in the upper chamber, where they were gathered together."

This was a night meeting - the dark part of the first day of the week. In Bible reckoning, the dark part of the day comes before the light part. Genesis 1:5 - "And God called the light Day, and the darkness He called Night. And the evening and the morning were the first day." The dark part comes first.

The Bible reckons a day from sunset to sunset.

The seventh day begins on sunset Friday evening. The first day of the week begins sunset Saturday evening.

Paul is together with his friends on the dark part of the first day of the week - Saturday night. This is a farewell get-together. He preached until midnight, when poor Eutychus falls out of the window. (Acts 20:9).

You can imagine how relieved they were when it was found that God spared his life. Verse eleven says that they talked 'till the break of day, and then Paul departed. Verse thirteen shows that Paul spent that Sunday morning traveling to Assos.

There's nothing here either concerning a change of the Sabbath.

The New English Bible translates this text like this: "On the Saturday night, in our assembly for the breaking of bread, Paul, who was to leave the next day, addressed them, and went on speaking until midnight." Acts 20:7.

The last text mentions the first day of the week in I Corinthians 16:1,2.

It says - "Now concerning the collection for the saints, as I have given order to the churches of Galatia, even so do ye. Upon the first day of the week let every one of you lay by him in store, as God hath prospered him, that there be no gatherings when I come." Verse three tells that he will bring the offering to Jerusalem.

As he had done in Galatia, so Paul also requests of those in Corinth to have a collection all ready when he would come to take it to the poor saints in Jerusalem. There's nothing in the text about a church service, but each person is to "lay by him in store." The first of the week was the best time for the people to set some money aside because later in the week, it would be spent. That's true today as well! Paul requested this so that "there be no gatherings when I come." I Corinthians 16:2.

At this time the Christians are suffering hardship in Jerusalem, and Paul is making his rounds to the churches taking up a collection for them. (We should be that thoughtful today.)

There's nothing in this text either about a change of God's Sabbath to Sunday.

Concerning worship, what was Paul's custom?

Here it is -

"And Paul, as his manner was, went in unto them, and three Sabbath days reasoned with them out of the scriptures." Acts 1 7:2.

Jesus, as our example, also had the custom of attending church on Saturday, the seventh day, as we see in Luke 4:16.

The great time prophecies of the Bible have all been fulfilled on schedule. Thus the accuracy and dependability of God's word are firmly established.

Appendix 11

THE CEREMONIAL LAW
AND
THE TWO COVENANTS

The distinction between the moral law of God {the ten commandments}, and the ceremonial law, is plain.

Look carefully at the differences in the two. The one, with animal sacrifices, was nailed to the cross. The other will stand forever.

10 Commandments	Ceremonial Law
1) Is called the "royal law." James 2:8	- 1) Is called the law "contained in ordinances." Ephesians 2:15.
2) Was spoken by God. Deuteronomy 4:12,13.	- 2) Was spoken by Moses. Leviticus. 1:1-3.
3) Was written with the finger of God. Exodus 31:18.	- 3) Was written by Moses in a book. II Chronicles 35:12.
4) Was placed in the ark. Exodus 40:20, Hebrews 9:4.	- 4) Was placed in the side of the ark. Deuteronomy 31:24-26.
5) Will "stand forever and ever." Psalms 111:7,8.	- 5) Was nailed to the cross. Colossians 2:14.
6) Was not destroyed by Christ. Matthew 5:17,18.	- 6) Was abolished by Christ. Ephesians 2:15.

The two great commandments are, "Thou shalt love the Lord thy God with all thy heart, and with all thy soul, and with all thy mind;" and the second great commandment is "Thou shalt love thy neighbor as thyself." God's ten commandments are hanging on these two. The first four commandments, {on the first table}, tell us how to love God with all our heart. (Have no other Gods, not worship images, not take God's name in vain, and remember His Sabbath day to keep it holy.) And the last six, {on the second table} deal with loving our neighbor as ourselves. (To honor our parents, not kill, not commit adultery, not steal, not lie, not covet.)

THE OLD AND NEW COVENANTS

The old covenant was ratified by the blood of animals (Exodus 24:5-8 and Hebrews 9:19,20) and based upon the promises of the people that they would keep God's law.

The new covenant, on the other hand, is based on God's promise to write His moral law of ten commandments in our hearts, and it was ratified with the blood of Christ. (Hebrews 8:10 and Jeremiah 3 1:33,34.)

Hebrews 8:10 - "For this is the covenant that I will make with the house of Israel after those days, saith the Lord; I will put my laws into their minds, and write them in their hearts: and I will be to them a God, and they shall be to me a people."

APPENDIX 12

(TIME NOT LOST)

It takes the earth exactly 365 days, 5 hours, 48 minutes, and 47.8 seconds to go around the sun. But there's no way to put that into any calendar, so our calendar is constantly being updated. That's why we have a "leap year." In 1582, astronomers discovered that the year was a little longer than 365 days, so they updated the calender, but the weekly cycle was not altered. They simply made Thursday the 4th to be followed by Friday the 15th. The calendar was updated without altering the weekly cycle in any way.

Here in our day, the "leap year" nicely updates the calendar every four years {and has for centuries}, but the days of the week have never been changed. It's exciting to know that not even a minute of time has been lost track of. Praise God!

There have been many ancient calendars. The first modern calendar, similar to ours, was put into use in 45 B.C. (before Christ) by Julius Caesar. The names of the days as we have them now were also used then.

Since the Babylonians worshiped the planets, many anciently began to call the days of the week by the names of those planets. The Hebrews and the Bible writers never did that. This is why, even though the names of the days as we have them {Sunday, Monday etc.} existed around the time of Christ, the Bible writers never referred to the days by these names.

The old Mithra religion from the time of Babylon and Persia led to the naming of the days after the planets. Zoroaster popularized the god Mithra in Persia about 630 B.C. Since Mithra was supposedly a god of great courage, the Roman soldiers became worshipers of it. In their travels they carried the idea of naming the days of the week after the planets, {among the Teutonic tribes} of

91

Germany. The Teutons substituted a few of their own gods instead of planets for the names of days. (This was before the time of Christ.) The names stuck, and we've had them ever since.

Below is a list of the Teutonic gods and the days of our week.

Sun-Sunday
Moon - Monday
Tiu - Tuesday
Woden - Wednesday
Thor - Thursday
Frigg - Friday
Seturn - Saturday

Though the calendar is constantly being updated to compensate for the 365 days, 5 hours, 48 minutes, and 47.8 seconds in the year, yet, the week of seven days has never been altered.

Historians writing before the time of Christ, have referred to "the day of the Sun' and "the day of Saturn."

Dr. W.W. Campbell, director of the Lick Observatory in Mount Hamilton, California assures us:

"The week of seven days has been in use ever since the days of Moses, and we have no reason for supposing that any irregularities have existed in the succession of the weeks and their days from that time to the present." D.W. Cross, *Your Amazing Calendar,* (Taunton: 1972) pp. 6,7.

Time can be traced to the very second by the positions of the stars! I wrote to the Pentagon in Washington D.C., the Department of Astronomy. I received a courteous letter.

The letter informed me that from the positions of the stars, every moment of time has been kept track of since before 500 B.C.

Dr. J.B. Dimbleby, premier chronologist to the British Chronological and Astronomical Association, after years of careful calculations asserts: "If men refused to observe weeks, and the line of time was forgotten, the day of the week could be recovered by observing when the transits of the planets, or eclipses of the Sun and Moon occurred. These great sentinels of the sky keep seven days with scientific accuracy, thundering out the seven days inscribed on the inspired page." *All Past Time,* p. 10.

It's interesting to note how Dr. G. E. Hale, noted astronomer for whom the great Palomar telescope has been named, expressed the same truth in five forceful words: "No time has been lost."

Bibliography

Chapter 1
1) Vandeman, George, *Destination Life*, (Mountain View Pacific Press Pub. Assoc., 1980), p. 74.
2) White, E.G., *Cosmic Conflict*, (Washington: Review & Herald Pub. Assoc., 1982), p. 388.
3) Ibid. p. 389.
4) *Violence and the Mass Media*, (New York: Harper & Row, 1968), p. 51.
5) Ibid. p. 43.
6) Life, January, 1988, p. 46.
7) Gulley, Norman, *Is the Majority Moral?*, (Washington: Review & Herald Pub. Assoc., 1981), p. 8.
8) Ibid.
9) Ibid. p. 10.
10) Ibid. p. 20.
11) Ibid.

Chapter 2
1) Smith, Uriah, *Daniel and the Revelation*, (Nashville: Southern Publishing Assoc., 1944), pp. 42, 43.
2) Ibld, p. 92.

Chapter 3
1) Stringfellow, Bill *All In the Name of the Lord*, (Clermont: Concerned Publications, 1981), p. 124.
2) White. E.G., *Cosmic Conflict*, (Washington: Review & Herald Pub. Assoc., 1982), pp. 38-40.

Chapter 4
1) White, E.G., *Cosmic Conflict*, (Washington: Review and Herald Pub. Assoc., 1982), p. 498.
2) *The Catholic Church, The Renaissance, and Protestantism*, p. 182, 183.
3) White, E.G., *Cosmic Conflict*, (Washington: Review & Herald Pub. Assoc., 1982), p. 72.
4) Catholic Mirror, September 23, 1893. (Official organ of Cardinal Gibbons).
5) Catholic Press, Sydney, Australia), August 25, 1900.

Chapter 5
1) Thomas, H.F., Chancellor of Cardinal Gibbons, (In answer to a letter regarding the change of the Sabbath).
2) Father Enright, C.S.S.R. of the Redemptoral College, Kansas City, MO., (*In History of the Sabbath*, p. 802).

Chapter 6
1) Stringfellow, Bill, *All In The Name Of The Lord*, (Clermont: Concerned Publications, 1981), pp. 134-135.
2) Catholic Twin Circle, August 25, 1985, Art. "Sacking Sunday."
3) Liberty Confidential Newsletter, Vol. 5, 1982.
4) These Times, April, 1982, Norman Gulley, "Life After Death – What About the New Evidence?"

Chapter 7
1) Olson, R.W., *The Crisis Ahead*, (Angwin: Pacific Union College Book Store, 1981), p. 5.
2) White, E.G., *Cosmic Conflict*, (Washington: Review & Herald Pub. Assoc., 1982), p. 557.
3) Ibid. pp. 558-561.
4) Ibid, pp. 561-566.